A Winter Dictionary

A Winter Dictionary

A collection of words for the festive season

Paul Anthony Jones

Elliott&Thompson

First published 2024 by
Elliott and Thompson Limited
2 John Street
London WC1N 2ES
www.eandtbooks.com

ISBN: 978-1-78396-823-7

9 8 7 6 5 4 3 2 1

A catalogue record for this book is available from the British Library.

Typesetting by Marie Doherty

Printed by CPI Group (UK) Ltd, Croydon, CR0 4YY

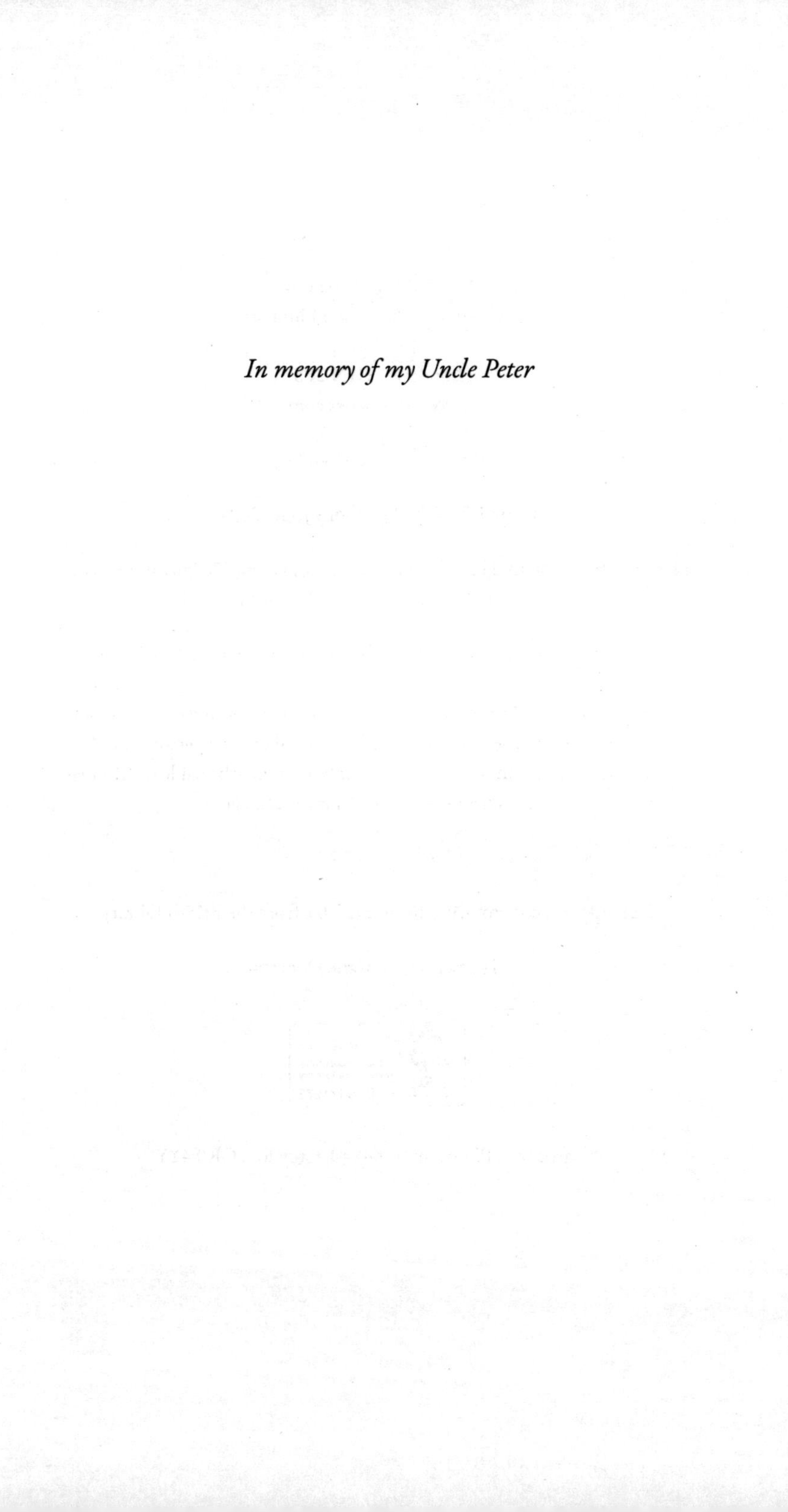

In memory of my Uncle Peter

CONTENTS

INTRODUCTION

There comes a moment each year – first thing in the morning, usually sometime in the middle of autumn – when you step outside and notice everything is suddenly and unexpectedly crisp. The sky is not quite as bright as it has been in recent days. A thin layer of dew has accumulated on every surface. There might be the slightest hint of a hazy bluish mist hanging in the air. The grass and the ground are speckled with ice and, as you walk, the brown and orange leaves under your feet crunch with the first frost of the season.

It's a familiar scene, and an equally familiar feeling – so much so, in fact, that over the passing centuries countless ingenious people have come up with words for these most recognisable moments of the oncoming winter. That hazy autumn mist, for instance, is a *blewse*. A dew-covered surface can be said to be *rorulent*, or *hammelled* if the moisture has begun to freeze. An early autumn frost is a *sniveler*, while frosty ground that crunches and crackles as you walk on it is *chibbly*. And the gradual diminishing of the daylight hours as the year nears its end can be known as *darkling*.

As autumn continues to give way to winter, a host of other cold-weather words come into play, such as a *frost-hag* (a freezing mist), *queeving* (the bending of treetops in the wind) and *foxing days* (on which the weather turns out better than it had promised earlier). When the temperatures drop and the ice and snow set in, you might find yourself *snerdling* (snuggling together for warmth), *peeling* (accidentally stepping out in insufficient clothing) or even *barflogging* (slapping your arms against your sides for warmth). Next comes the holiday season, when houses are *bouned* (decorated in evergreens), we all fall guilty of *abligurition* (profligate spending on food and drink) and at long last we can *powl* (leave work early to go to the pub) and enjoy a *kirsmas-glass* (a yuletide toast). And as the festivities wind down and the *barrel-sickness* (drunken overindulgence) starts to subside, the new year comes and goes and the world outside changes once again. Nature begins to *whicken* (awaken from the depths of winter), birds *valentine* (chirrup romantically) and, as the springtime approaches at last, you might experience your first *greenout* of the new year (the heart-lifting moment when you spy the first fresh green growth poking out above the wintry ground).

It is unusual and long-forgotten words just like these – over 400 of them, in fact – that have been collected here in *A Winter Dictionary*. Together these words cover more than one thousand years of the English language, from the very earliest Old English texts to contemporary coinages and modern slangy inventions, providing us with a robust (if largely overlooked) wintertime vocabulary. Practically all corners of the English-speaking world are namechecked along the way here, from Britain's patchwork of regional dialects to American and Canadian English, and even the only recently described jargon of polar researchers in Antarctica. A handful of notable words from languages outside of England have made these pages too – as well as several from the endlessly inventive and evocative language of Scots.

Some of these words are considered rather formal and literary, others scholarly and scientific, and many are squarely limited to regional dialects or local idiom, and have scarcely ever been heard or used outside of their home turf. Despite their relative obscurity, however, they have all been dutifully recorded and defined in the dictionaries and glossaries of the past by authors who noted their worth and sought to record their meaning and use for posterity as a result. These words might never have gained quite the level of use required to graduate onto the pages of the household dictionary on your bookshelf, of course, but that is not to say that they did not once (or, in many instances, still do) have sufficient circulation to warrant our attention.

Although this is first and foremost a dictionary, the words here have been organised into thematic chapters taking us right through the winter season – starting with those relating to the change from autumn into winter, and ending with the opposite change from winter into spring. The entries within each chapter are then listed alphabetically and dealt with as they would be in a standard dictionary, with a short definition followed by some explanatory notes on their history, origins, background and use. Any words in **bold type** can be cross-referenced and found elsewhere in this book; outside of each chapter, head to the Word Finder at the back to find your way around.

The date given in each entry represents the earliest independent written record of the word in question, used in the context given in the definition, that I have been able to track down. Unfortunately these dates are often very difficult to ascertain reliably (especially with dialect terms and inventions that may well have been in spoken use locally for centuries before finding their way into print). As a result, in many instances they should be taken only as an estimate, providing a rough guide to a word's age or to the era in which it first emerged. (If you have earlier evidence of a word than I have been able to track down here, of course, I'd be delighted to hear about it!)

Paul Anthony Jones

ABBREVIATIONS AND SYMBOLS USED IN THIS BOOK

?	denotes an approximate date or period, or an unclear or suggested etymology
<	derived from, descended from
adj.	adjective
adv.	adverb
app.	apparently
dial.	dialect
Dut.	Dutch
excl.	exclamation
Fr.	French
Ger.	German
Gk.	Greek
Icel.	Icelandic
Ir.	Irish
It.	Italian
Jap.	Japanese
Lat.	Latin
lit.	literally
ME	Middle English
n.	noun
naut.	nautical
Nor.	Norwegian
nr.	near
OE	Old English
ON	Old Norse
orig.	originally
phr.	phrase
pl.	plural
rel.	related to
Sc.	Scots
Scan.	Scandinavian

sl.	slang
Sp.	Spanish
Sw.	Swedish
v.	verb

1. THE CHANGING SEASONS

In the northern hemisphere at least, winter begins at the winter solstice when the Earth reaches its maximum tilt on its axis and so slants our part of the world to its furthest point away from the sun. We experience this as the shortest day of the year – around 21 or 22 December – after which the three long months of winter officially commence.

On a more personal scale, we will have felt the oncoming winter for a fair few weeks before this. The leaves on the trees change colour and then fall. Birds that only spend the summer with us prepare to migrate, and then depart. The winds pick up, the rain starts to fall, and day by day the temperatures cool and the turbulent skies darken. The very first wintry nip in the air is usually felt when the calendar tells us it is still autumn.

This period of change and seasonal upheaval is the subject of this first set of wintertime words, from the increasingly stormy weather to the jittery behaviour of our migratory wildlife.

abscission (*n.*) the process by which a leaf detaches from its tree in autumn [1887; < Lat. *abscindere*, 'to cut off, to separate']

In general terms *abscission* is just the act of detaching or cutting something away, and in the five centuries or so that the word has been in use it has been applied to everything from surgical procedures to religious excommunication. In botanical terms, though, *abscission* is the natural shedding of a part of a plant or tree – like a ripened fruit, a flower lost after pollination or a withered autumn leaf. The precise point at which a leaf breaks away from its tree is called the *abscission zone*.

See also **marcescent**

afterlight (*n.*) the glow that remains in the sky after the sun has set [1683]

As the sun's rays begin to fade a little earlier each day in the autumn, you might find yourself still busy out of doors or on your way home with only their *afterlight* in the sky.

> *The evening of the year! . . . The hours wane quickly into shadow, and a chilliness as of the night wind is upon the earth. Sometimes a summer day peeps in here and there like the after-light of the sun, but its aspect is out of season, and it greets us with a melancholy beauty.*
> E. H. Chapin, 'Seasons of Meditation', *The Rose of Charon* (1850)

akering-time (*n.*) the autumn; in particular, the period in late autumn when oak trees start to drop their acorns [dial., 1883; < *aker*, 'acorn']

The 'akering' here is just a dialect alteration of *acorning*, the collecting or gathering of acorns, which have long been used as meal to fatten pigs ahead of the winter. Likewise, *akermast* is the collective name for all the fallen fruit of an oak tree lying on the forest floor.

backendish (*adj.*) of the weather, rough and stormy [dial., 1898; < *back end*, 'the rearmost part' + *–ish*]

A word used to describe weather that seems quite literally appropriate for the 'back end' of the year – so something well worth remembering in the ever wetter and windier final weeks of autumn. Or, in Britain at least, much of the rest of the year.

big eye (*n.*) sleeplessness or insomnia, caused or worsened by changes in the length of the day [1958; ? < the wide open eyes of a sleepless person]

This twentieth-century coinage was invented by insomniac polar scientists struggling to deal with the extreme and prolonged changes of night and day in Antarctica. The seasonal change might not be quite so severe in our part of the world, but it can still be discombobulating to find the sky completely dark at four o'clock in the afternoon (and still just as dark at eight o'clock the following morning).

blewse (*n.*) a bluish morning's mist [dial., 1887; < 'blues']

Seemingly nothing more than a dialect adjustment of 'blues', *blewse* mists are apparently common in the late summer and early autumn when, as a sign of things to come, the temperature suddenly drops overnight following a cloudlessly sunny day.

> *Blewse . . . A bluish mist, not unusual in summer when the temperature suddenly becomes chilled, the sky remaining cloudless. It is supposed to bring a blight.*
>
> F. B. Zincke, *Some Materials for the History of Wherstead* (1887)

chirming (*n.*, *v.*) the subdued twittering of birds before a storm [dial., 1846; < OE *cirm*]

The intermingled sound of different birds' songs has been known as *chirming* since Old English times, but by the nineteenth century the more specific and more evocative meaning above had emerged in a handful of English dialects. 'The melancholy under-tone of a bird previous to a storm' is how one Victorian dictionary defined a *chirm*, making this the perfect word for the restless and eerily restrained chirruping of birds as they are forced to take shelter during the squally autumn months.

corner-frost (*n.*) a very faint or early frost, occurring outside of or long before the wintertime [1898]

An unseasonably early or only very slight frost can be known as a *corner-frost* because it might just succeed in freezing the very corners of a field or garden, or touch upon only the most exposed parts of a landscape.

cosmognosis (*n.*) the instinctive force that tells an animal when and where to migrate [1882; < Gk. *cosmos*, 'the world, the universe' + *gnosis*, 'knowledge']

Built from a pair of Greek roots that together literally mean a 'knowledge of the world', *cosmognosis* was coined in the mid 1800s, at a time when many of the precise details of animal migration were still largely unknown. For centuries the annual disappearance of migratory animals had been accounted for by all manner of elaborate theories: the departure of swallows in the autumn, for instance, was variously ascribed to the birds flying far out to sea, hibernating at the bottom of ponds and even escaping to the moon to avoid the winter weather. We might know more about migration today, but quite what prompts migratory creatures to begin their journeys when the seasons change – the enigmatic instinct encapsulated in the word *cosmognosis* – remains something of a mystery.

See also **zeitgeber**, **zugunruhe**

cyclonopathy (*n.*) an abnormal sensitivity to changing weather conditions [1958; < *cyclono–*, *cyclone*, 'great storm' (< Gk. *cyclos*, 'wheel') + *–pathy*, 'feeling, disease' (< Gk. *pathos*, 'suffering')]

'Discomfort felt by some people [*on the*] approach of unpleasant weather' is how one 1950s medical dictionary defined this word, although whether *cyclonopathy* and the associated **meteorotropism** and **ombrosalgia** are genuine medical conditions at all is a controversial subject. There is certainly plenty of anecdotal evidence to suggest some of us are indeed laid low by seasonal changes in the atmosphere, and not just in the wintertime either. In Argentina, a dry and dusty wind known as the *zonda* is said to bring such terrible sleeplessness and depressiveness down the eastern slopes of the Andes that it is known locally as 'the witch's wind'. New Zealand's strong *nor'wester* gales have been linked to seasonal increases in everything from violent behaviour to anxiety. And so many people report feeling out of sorts when the local *foehn* winds blow down the northern slopes of the Swiss Alps that the widespread malaise they are said to bring with them has been known as *föhnkrankheit*, or 'foehn sickness', for well over a century. Even the great Joan Didion once wrote of her and her Los Angeles neighbours' seemingly preternatural ability to forecast the arrival of California's Santa Ana winds every autumn:

> *I have neither heard nor read that a Santa Ana is due, but I know it, and almost everyone I have seen today knows it too. We know it because we feel it. The baby frets. The maid sulks. I rekindle a waning argument with the telephone company, then cut my losses and lie down, given over to whatever it is in the air.*
>
> Joan Didion, 'The Santa Anas', *Slouching Towards Bethlehem* (1969)

darkle (*v.*) to become gradually darker, as the days towards the end of the year [1868; apparently < earlier adv. *darkling*, 'in the dark' (*c.* 15thC)]

This excellent word is an example of a back-formation – a word effectively coined in reverse. In medieval English, *darkling* meant hidden or concealed, or quite literally 'in the dark'. In the 1500s, however, it was mistakenly interpreted as a verb (thanks to its *–ing* ending), and so *darkle* fell into occasional use as its supposed root.

Over the centuries that followed, *darkle* was applied in an array of different literal and figurative darkening contexts, and variously used to mean to hide in the dark, to grimace or show anger in your face, to come into view only slightly or indistinctly, and – in the early 1800s – to grow or to gradually become dark. As well as describing the darkening of the sky towards evening and nightfall, finally *darkle* also came to be used of the even more gradual darkening of the days as the year approaches its end and winter slowly starts to creep in.

Look around and lift thy heart
To take a thankful part
In nature's mellow chorus;
Those tinted trees and bushes say
We need not send our joys away,
Tho' darkling winter be before us.

Saumarez Smith, 'Autumn Tints' (1868)

erythrophyll (*n.*) a natural pigment that turns leaves red in autumn [1843; < *erythro–* (< Gk. *erythros*, 'red') + *–phyll* (< Gk. *phyllon*, 'leaf')]

See **xanthophyll**

farewell summer (*n.*) the robin [1884]

Robins are not migratory birds, but as this term suggests their association with the festive period has led to them being seen in some people's eyes as symbols not just of the winter, but of the end of summer too. According to folklore, moreover, a robin hopping over the threshold of your home forecasts a snap of cold and wintry weather ahead.

See also **farewell fieldfare**

filemot (*n.*) the colour of a dead or dying leaf [*c.* 1640; < Fr. *feuillemorte*, 'dead leaf']

Both *filemot* and the original French term from which it is derived, *feuillemorte*, have been in occasional use in English to describe the colour of dead leaves since the seventeenth century at least.

Hollantide (*n.*) the first week of November [1573; < lit. 'All Hallows' Tide']

Etymologically, *Hollantide* is All Hallows' Tide – that is, the period around All Saints' Day, 1 November. According to traditional folklore, if rivers and duck ponds freeze over during Hollantide, then winter has struck too early and they will be ice-free by Christmas Day.

gab (*n.*) a spell of wintry weather when it is still autumn [Sc., 1916; < *gab o' winter*, lit. 'the opening of winter' < *gab*, 'mouth']

Gab, like *gob*, has been used to mean a mouth since the seventeenth century, but its etymological roots run far deeper than that. Similar words in Scots, Irish and even Gaulish suggest this was likely an ancient Celtic word for a mouth, or a bird's beak.

It is in the literal sense of an 'opening' (and therefore, a beginning) that *gab* later came to be used of a so-called *gab o' winter* – a period of unseasonably early cold weather that strikes in the autumn, giving an unwelcome foretaste of what lies ahead.

go-harvest (*n.*) the late autumn, the changeable period between harvest time and the start of winter; a period of warm weather in early November [dial., 1735; ? < *gossamer*, lit. 'goose summer' + *harvest*, 'harvest time, the autumn season']

There is a rather convoluted etymological story to unpack here involving geese, spider's silk and manmade fabrics. The tale begins in medieval Europe, where a 'goose summer' was a period of unseasonably warm weather around the time of St Martin's Day, 11 November, when geese were said to be in best season. 'Goose summer' reduced to *gossamer* over time, and with it the word's meaning shifted, eventually coming to refer to the dewy masses of spider's silk often seen on tufts of grass at this time of year. From there, it was only an etymological hop, skip and jump to *gossamer* becoming the name of an equally silken gauze-like fabric in the early 1800s.

In Scots and a handful of northern dialects of English, meanwhile, 'goose summer' took a different route and was cut down to *go-summer*. Seemingly under the misapprehension that this must somehow derive from 'summer' (rather than autumn) and 'go' (rather than 'goose'), a new term, *go-harvest*, fell into use in the 1700s as a more explicitly autumnal name for this period of warm, summer-like weather at the end of the year.

lecking-time (*n.*) a day or period of alternating sunshine and rain showers [dial., 1830; < *leck*, 'to sprinkle with water' ? < *leak*]

Likely derived from *leak*, to *leck* or *lech* something is to splash or sprinkle it with water, so a *lecking-day* or *lecking-time* is a frustratingly changeable day on which every so often the weather decides to do just that.

marcescent (*adj.*) descriptive of a leaf that withers and dies in the autumn, but remains attached to its tree [1727; < Lat. *marcere*, 'to wither, to shrivel']

A dead leaf resolutely clinging to its otherwise bare tree is a *marcescent* leaf. Sometimes this is merely an isolated anomaly, but some trees intentionally retain almost all their leaves in a marcescent state throughout the winter, perhaps as a means of shielding their bark and their branches from grazing animals, or else to give their delicate buds and new growth some much-needed protection come the springtime.

The word *marcescent* itself comes from the Latin verb *marcere*, meaning to wither. If you're feeling a little withered and run down by the winter months yourself, then helpfully that word is also the origin of the adjective *marcid*, meaning faint, feeble or exhausted.

See also **abscission**

***momijigari* (*n.*) the Japanese custom of visiting forests in autumn to look at the changing foliage [< Jap. *momiji*, 'red leaves' + *gari*, 'hunting']**

Momijigari is essentially a far more exquisite-sounding equivalent of what might otherwise (in American English at least) be better known as 'leaf-peeping'. A similar Japanese custom that could likewise come in handy at this time of year is *shinrinyoku*: a word for a relaxing trip to a forest taken to improve your health and wellbeing, it literally means 'forest-bathing'.

queeving (*n.*, *v.*) the gentle bending back and forth of trees in the wind [dial., 1809; < *queeve*, 'to bend']

As the autumn winds start to pick up, it is the *queeving* of the trees that gently shakes the dry leaves from their branches. As a verb, *queeve* is recorded in a handful of English dialects in a variety of senses (to bend, to twist, to tremble, to vibrate, to move to and fro), all essentially relating to some kind of backward-and-forward motion. The rather more specific definition above is just one of these, listed in a guide to the dialect of Bedfordshire back in 1809.

rorulent (*adj.*) coated in dew [1656; < Lat. *rorulentus*, 'dewy' < *ros*, 'dew']

English has a surprisingly large number of dew-dappled words like this one, including *roriferous* (producing dew), *rorifluent* (flowing with dew) and *rorigenous* (produced by dew). All of them ultimately come from the Latin word for dew, *ros* – which, despite appearances, makes them all etymological cousins of the herb rosemary. A reference to the plant's apparent ability to survive on nothing more than coastal mist and condensation, the name *rosemary* comes from the Latin *rosmarinus*, literally meaning 'dew of the sea'.

seasonal polyphenism (*n.*) the outward transformation of an animal in response to the changing seasons [< *polyphenism*, 1963 < *poly–*, 'many' + *phenotype* (< Gk. *phaino*, 'to cause to appear') + *–ism*]

Polyphenism is a curious biological phenomenon that allows multiple different forms (or *phenotypes*) of a species to develop from the same genetic makeup (or *genotype*), with these different forms produced as a result of environmental rather than genetic factors. What does all of that mean? Well, in nature these changes are borne out in all manner of different ways, from the sex of turtle hatchlings (which is determined by the temperature at which the eggs develop) to the social systems of ants (in which a single egg can turn into a worker, a soldier or a queen, depending on which is most in demand at the time). *Seasonal polyphenism* is the specific name given to another form of this kind of variation, in which a creature is able to alter its outward appearance, often drastically, in response to the time of year, while remaining genetically unchanged. It is this, ultimately, that accounts for the likes of stoats, hares and ptarmigan birds turning pure white ahead of the snowy winter months.

scuppered (*adj.*) of leaves, curled or blighted with frost [dial., 1847; ? < *scupper*, 'to ruin']

Scuppers are the openings in the side of a ship that allow any water thrown up onto the deck to run back into the sea. Whether they are related to the verb *scupper*, meaning to ruin, is unclear; in this sense, *scupper* is a Britishism not much heard elsewhere in the English-speaking world, which emerged in the early 1800s as military slang for a surprise attack. Whether there is any connection between either of these *scuppers* and the wintry adjective *scuppered* is likewise unclear – though from the point of view of a keen gardener, it is easy to imagine how an equally keen frost might 'scupper' an otherwise healthy autumn harvest.

sniveler (*n.*) a light frost in the early autumn [dial., 1904; < *snivel*, 'to sniffle, to breathe through a congested nose' < OE *snyflan*]

People have been *snivelling* when they have a runny nose since the very earliest days of Old English. Fast-forward a few centuries, and in the early 1800s a *sniveler*, or *sniveller*, was both a sharp, chilling breeze (just the kind that might cause a person's nose to run) and 'a slight hoar-frost in early autumn', according to the *English Dialect Dictionary*.

St Andrew's blast (*n.*) a period of late autumn frost and snow that tends to fall around St Andrew's Day [1904; < *St Andrew*, patron saint of Scotland + *blast* < OE *blæst*, 'gust of wind']

The very earliest meaning of *blast* in English relates to the weather; in Old English a *blæst* was a strong gale or gust of wind (while the word itself is likely a very distant etymological cousin of the verb *blow*). All other uses of *blast* – an explosion, a loud noise, a riotously good time – are later developments and metaphors.

According to folklore, not only can you expect a blast of wintry weather around St Andrew's Day, 30 November, but you can use the day itself to forecast the weather for the year to come. Place a tumbler of water, full to the brim, on a table on St Andrew's Day, and if a single drop spills down the side, then you can supposedly expect the following year to be something of a washout. If the table remains dry, then so too will the year ahead.

swallow storms (*n. pl.*) periods of rough and windy weather around early October [dial., 1877]

Swallow storms are so called because they are traditionally said to blow in around the same time that the swallows that have spent the summer in the British Isles have the sense to depart for warmer climes ahead of the winter. The same storms can then be expected to blow in again in the middle of springtime the following year, when the swallows return.

See also **chelidonian**

thunder-drop (*n.*) one of the large, widely dispersed raindrops that fall at the very beginning of a thunderstorm [1832]

Thundery downpours are by no means exclusive to autumn (not least in the British Isles), but as the weather begins to turn wetter and more unsettled, this may well be a term that finds increased currency towards the end of the year.

Her slow full words sank thro' the silence drear,
As thunder-drops fall on a sleeping sea;
Sudden I heard a voice that cried, 'Come here,
That I may look on thee.'

Alfred, Lord Tennyson, 'A Dream of Fair Women' (1833)

water-dog (*n.*) a small grey raincloud hanging below a larger white cloud [1830; < *water* + *dog*, recorded as a nickname for various weather phenomena since the 1600s]

Like Inuit words for snow, so are the dialects of English chock-full of words to describe the shape, form and portentousness of different cloud formations. *Water-dog* is just one of them – and, for that matter, one that is apparently commonest in the ever more unsettled skies of autumn. According to folklore, moreover, water-dogs are said to portend harsher or wetter conditions to come:

Water-dogs [are] ... *small clouds of irregular but roundish form, and of a darker colour, floating below the dense mass of cloudiness in rainy seasons, supposed to indicate the near approach of more rain.*

Robert Forby, *The Vocabulary of East Anglia* (1830)

wederognomonia (*n.*) a person's apparent ability to use their bodily aches and pains to predict rough or changeable weather to come [1958; < *weder*, 'weather' + Gk. *gnomon*, 'indicator, interpreter' < *gignosco*, 'to understand']

See **cyclonopathy**

wedge (*n.*) the V-shaped line formed by geese in flight [1869]

A flock of geese is known as a *gaggle* when on the ground, but it becomes a *skein* as soon as the birds take flight, typically forming a characteristic V-shape or *wedge* in the air. In fact, it is the long, trailing lines of birds that make up the wedge that are the reason for the change of name here, as the geese in flight are imaginatively said to resemble a strand of yarn being unwound from a skein of wool.

xanthophyll (*n.*) a yellowish pigment found in leaves that becomes visible in the autumn [1838; < *xantho–* (< Gk. *xanthos*, 'yellow') + *–phyll* (< Gk. *phyllon*, 'leaf')]

When the seasons change, the chlorophyll that ordinarily gives leaves their greenish hue starts to break down, giving other colours and pigments inside each leaf the chance to shine through instead. Among them are *xanthophyll*, which gives autumn leaves their yellowish hue, and **erythrophyll**, which turns them red.

zeitgeber (*n.*) a regular environmental event that keeps an organism's biological clock in time [1971; < Ger. *Zeit*, 'time' + *Geber*, 'giver, donor']

All creatures have an inbuilt clock around which their regular natural activities, such as sleeping and eating, are synchronised. This internal clock is in turn kept in check by external events – like the rising and setting of the sun – known as *zeitgebers*, or literally 'time-givers'. Different creatures work to different schedules, of course, so while we humans mostly rely on the so-called 'circadian' cycle of night and day every twenty-four hours, animals living by the seashore might operate around the twice-daily ebb and flow of the tide, for instance. In creatures that hibernate or migrate, it is the changing of the seasons that acts as their zeitgeber, prompting them to make all the necessary preparations in the autumn to ensure their safety and survival over the winter.

zugunruhe (*n.*) the restlessness of migratory birds ahead of their departure [1707; < Ger. *Zug*, 'migration, movement' + *Unruhe*, 'restlessness, anxiousness']

If you're a **cyclonopath** who finds yourself feeling increasingly restless during the changing of the seasons, then you're by no means alone. Adopted into English from German, the word *zugunruhe* (literally, 'migration anxiety') refers to the tense, jittery behaviour commonly seen in birds as they prepare for migration. This phenomenon was first observed in the early eighteenth century by biologists who noted that captive birds in zoos and private collections could not overcome their natural instinct to migrate, despite being confined to a cage and therefore unable to embark on the annual journeys they seemed so restlessly hardwired to complete.

See also **cosmognosis**

2. WINTER STORMS

After a few weeks or months of autumnal restlessness, the winter finally arrives when the weather breaks, the temperatures plunge and the snowstorms blow in. It is a cold and bleak time of year, but there is at least one silver lining: now, we all get to talk about it.

Research has shown that nine out of ten British people will have spoken to someone about the weather within the last six hours (while around a third will have talked about it in the last sixty minutes). In fact, a survey published in 2015 found that Brits will on average spend around four months of their entire lives making meteorological small talk. It is perhaps for good reason, then, that our weather-related vocabulary is enormously well furnished.

There are so many words relating to the worst of the winter weather in particular that they're split up between the next two chapters here. This chapter relates to the wind, rain, mist, fog and thick cloud that tend to characterise a typical British winter's day, while the freezing temperatures and ice and snow of our more traditional idea of wintertime make up the chapter that follows. Feel free to drop any one of these words into your next conversation – which, if research is to be believed, should come along in about half an hour or so.

bange (*n.*) a drizzling mist [dial., 1839 ? < Fr. *baigner*, 'to bathe']

bangy (*adj.*) drizzly; stormy, overcast [dial., 1790]

There is an etymological chicken-and-egg problem lurking behind this pair of drizzly words from the dialects of southeast England.

On the one hand, the written evidence suggests that the adjective *bangy* came first, sometime in the late 1700s, and that the noun *bange* was clipped from that after the turn of the century. Despite that, however, a more plausible explanation would be that *bange* was actually the earlier word, and bange-like weather came to be labelled as *bangy* as a result of that. No matter what way round the words fell into use, in the sense of slowly becoming thoroughly wet through in grim, drizzly weather, it has been suggested that both might somehow be distantly related to *baigner*, the French word for bathe.

doggindales (*n. pl.*) patches of mist that cling to sheltered hillsides [Sc., dial., 1866; ? < *donkindale*, lit. 'dank in the dale']

Nothing to do with dogs, alas, this word is probably a Scots or northern English dialect alteration of a 'dank in the dale'; a Northumberland equivalent was a *donkindale*, defined as a kind of 'raw mist on the water' or 'humidity rising in the evening in the hollow parts of meadows', according to one 1892 dictionary. *Doggindales* themselves, meanwhile, 'are looked upon as a sign of southerly winds'.

dooming (*n.*) the falling of mist or low cloud onto the land [dial., 1900; ? < dial. *doom*, 'dumb']

This fateful-sounding word – recorded as a Devon dialect term presumably in use since the nineteenth century at least – might appear as if it should be ominously related to the word *doom*, but a more likely theory is that it comes from *dumb*, perhaps in the figurative sense of thick cloud or fog deadening and muting the world around it.

driffle (*n.*) a slight, stormy shower of rain or snow [Sc., 1825; ? < rel. *drive*]

As a verb, to *driffle* or *dreefle* can also be used to mean to rain or snow only very lightly. As a noun, meanwhile, the same word can be used not only of a short or light spell of rough weather, but more figuratively of a hastily completed task or rush-job.

drow (*n.*) a cold mist, heavy or damp enough to almost feel like rain [Sc., 1818; of unknown origin, ? < *drown*]

'A cold mist approaching to rain' is how the great Scots lexicographer John Jamieson defined a *drow* back in 1825. Taking its name from an apparently frequently mist-filled valley in Roxburghshire, meanwhile, a *Liddisdale drow* in particular is 'a shower that wets an Englishman to the skin'.

fogbow (*n.*) a colourless rainbow produced by sunlight shining through mist or fog [1820; < *fog* + *bow* (< *rainbow*)]

The water droplets in mist or fog are far smaller than the raindrops that ordinarily produce rainbows, so the sunlight shining through them is not split up into a spectrum. As a result, the 'bow' that the sunlight creates as it passes through the droplets is almost entirely colourless.

foxing day (*n.*) a day on which the weather turns out better than it seemed it would [1895; < *fox*, 'to deceive, to get the better of']

A meteorologically 'deceitful day' is how one dictionary defined this quaint nineteenth-century invention. The same definition also explained that in the sense of a finer day that brings respite amid a period of rougher weather, the name *foxing day* can be applied to a brief but welcome lull in a storm.

frost-hag (*n.*) a freezing mist [dial., 1855; < *frost* + *hag*, 'a thick mist' (18thC)]

The word *hag* has been used to mean a thick white mist or fog since the mid eighteenth century at least, making a *frost-hag* an especially cold mist that appears to freeze all that it touches, leaving a thick white hoar frost behind it.

gramshoch (*n.*) the kind of tumultuous appearance of the sky or cloud that suggests a snowstorm is on its way [Sc., 1825; ? < Sc. *gram*, 'fierce']

The origins of this excellent Scots word are somewhat unclear: even the *Scottish National Dictionary* labels it as 'rather suspect'. If not related in some way to *gram*, an older Scots word meaning fierce or angry, the root here could instead be *ramsh*, meaning rough or coarse.

hemel (*n.*) a freezing fog [dial., 1897; of unknown origin]

'During the whole of this week the weather on Dartmoor has been very severe,' complained an article in the *Western Morning News* back in 1897. 'On Wednesday the cold was intense, and the frozen fog (locally known as 'hemel') caused the paths and roads to become very slippery and dangerous to pedestrians.'

See also **hammelled**

hunch-weather (*n.*) weather cold or unpleasant enough to make people walk with hunched shoulders [1846]

See **hirple, hurple**

mirkabrod (*n.*) a thin, patchy hillside mist [Sc., 1908; < ON *myrkr*, 'darkness' + *brot*, 'fragment']

Admittedly, labelling this as a Scots word is not entirely accurate, as it is more specifically from Norn, an ancient Norse-influenced language once spoken in Shetland and Orkney. At its roots lie two Old Norse words meaning darkness, *myrkr*, and a small broken fragment, *brot* – giving us a wonderfully evocative term for a mirky, moody, hillside mist.

mist-fawn (*n.*) a low-lying, isolated patch of white mist [Sc., 1825; ? < *fawn*, 'pale patch of moorland']

Although the Scots lexicographer John Jamieson somewhat dismissively called this 'a word formed from fancy', *fawn* is an earlier Scots term used of any noticeably pale patch of heathy or moss-covered land. Perhaps, then, this word is a subtle reference to a patch of similarly noticeable pale white mist disconnected from all around it.

moonbrough (*n.*) a halo-like circle of mist or cloud surrounding the moon [dial., 1899; *moon* + *brough*, 'halo of haze' (< ON *borg*, 'encircling wall')]

In the cold, clear skies of winter, the moon may well appear to shine through an encircling misty halo of cloud or fog. Derived from an ancient Scandinavian word for a surrounding wall or fortified enclosure, *brough* or *broch* has been used to refer to a hazy glowing circle of cloud – around either the sun or the moon – since the fifteenth century at least.

> *Halos round the sun or moon (called sun or moon brochs) were unwelcome sights, and were anxiously watched . . . [I]f the halo disappears before sunset, the sun is likely to rise in a clear sky, and the following day will be fair.*
> John Spence, *Shetland Folklore* (1899)

open-weather (*n.*) calm, clear winter weather, neither frosty nor snowy [orig. naut., 17thC; < *open*, 'free of obstacles']

Open-weather was originally a maritime term used of the kind of calm or 'open' conditions at sea that allow a vessel effortless passage to the shore. In winter, and not necessarily out at sea, the same term can be used of equally calm and clear conditions that are noticeably devoid of any of the unpleasant wintertime weather features, like sleet, ice and snow.

peel-a-bone, peel-the-bones (*n.*) extremely cold wintry weather; a piercing chilly wind [dial., 1824; < *peel*, 'to cut away or remove an outer layer']

See **peel**

pell (*n.*) a heavy, windy shower of rain and hail [dial., 1852; < *pell*, 'to dash, to strike']

As a verb, *pell* has been used since medieval times to mean to strike or beat down violently. Its use as a noun for a similarly heavy storm appears to have been a later development, found in print from the mid 1800s: 'A heavy shower of rain or hail, accompanied with a strong wind' is how the *English Dialect Dictionary* defined this in 1903.

rack (*n.*) a fast-moving bank of mist or cloud, especially one moving distinctly alongside a slower or stationary one [dial., ? 14thC; orig. 'rapid movement', of unknown origin]

The precise history of this word is somewhat cloudy (appropriately enough), with no clear explanation of where or how it first emerged some 600 years ago or so. What we do know is that its original meaning – any rapid, headlong movement – was a far more general one, and this specific reference to a fast-moving bank of mist or cloud was likely a later development. Nevertheless, by the mid nineteenth century this meteorological meaning had established itself in a handful of northern English and Scottish dialects, variously defined as wispy wind-driven clouds, fast-flying clouds in the upper atmosphere or a distinct pattern or layer of clouds moving separately from all the others around it. The vague course or direction the clouds take across the sky, meanwhile, has been known as 'the rack of the weather' since the 1700s.

roke (*n.*) a cold, damp, low-lying morning mist; a seaborne mist that precedes stormy weather [*c.* 15thC; < ON, ? rel. *roka*, 'fine sea spray']

Thought to have its roots in Scandinavia, the word *roke* dates back as far as the 1200s in English, when it was originally applied to smoke or vapour. The meteorological sense developed from there, and the word was for several centuries used somewhat loosely of any smoke-like mass of mist, cloud, fog or drizzling rain. The rather more specific use of *roke* (or *rawk*, or *roak* for that matter) to mean a fine, low-lying morning mist – and in particular one driven inland from the sea, ahead of a storm – appears to have developed in a handful of the weather-beaten dialects of England's North Sea coast.

skiting (*n.*, *v.*) the rebounding of hailstones as they strike a hard surface [? 18thC; < dial. *skite*, 'to move quickly, to move in leaps and bounds']

Just like similar words such as *skit* and *skitter*, *skite* has long been used to mean to move with great speed or force, before a secondary sense of a rebounding or ricocheting movement – and in particular that of hail or hard rain – emerged in Scots and some northern dialects of English around the early eighteenth century. (Just be careful not to mix this one up with the Scandinavian-origin verb *skite*, or *skyte*, which in the words of the *Oxford English Dictionary* means 'to void excrement'.)

slobber (*n.*) sleety rain [dial., 1879; < *slobber*, 'mud, slime']

The word *slobber* originally meant wet mud or ooze when it first appeared in the language in the mid 1400s. Over the five centuries or so since, it has gone on to pick up a number of equally unpleasant and unseemly meanings, including animal entrails, gelatinous gruel, saliva or drool (the most common meaning today) and – in the mid nineteenth century or thereabouts – a cold, wet, sleety mixture of wet snow and rain.

smur (*n.*) a fine drizzle [dial., 1808; ? < Sc. *smore*, 'to smother, to cover entirely']

For such an unassuming word, *smur* has a plethora of recorded meanings, of which this is only the earliest. Elsewhere, *smur*, *smir* or *smoor*, as it can also be spelled, can be applied to a fine, light rain shower, thick falling snow, a dust cloud, a visibly moving mass of mist or fog, a shower of rain in summertime or a whirling fall of sleet. Despite such a vast body of recorded use, however, the word's precise origins are something of a mystery.

wallowish (*adj.*) wet and sleety wintry weather, where there is neither a thaw nor a frost [1846; < *wallow*, 'to indulge unrestrainedly']

When the winter weather seems to 'wallow' in an insipid and undecided no-man's-land of endless rain and sleet rather than ice and snow, then it is being decidedly *wallowish*.

wittewijven (*n. pl.*) individual wisps of mist, especially in graveyards [Dut.; lit. 'white women']

In Dutch folklore, the *Wittewijven*, or *Witte Wieven* ('white women'), are ancient wise women or seeresses, variously credited with the ability to cure all ills, using diverse herbal remedies, and to predict the future with wild prophecies. According to the mythology surrounding them, when one of the *Wittewijven* died, her spirit lived on in the earth surrounding the site of her grave. An individual wisp of mist or fog – especially on a hillside or in a graveyard – is ultimately said to show one of the *Wittewijven* rising from the dead, ready to provide help or prophecy to anyone who may need it once again.

3. ICE AND SNOW

Winter really is the season that keeps on giving when it comes to the weather. Just when you think it must have reached its peak with all the wind and rain, the temperatures drop and ice and snow set in instead. From crackling frosts to clumsy falls on frozen ground, the words in this chapter cover the very coldest of what the winter season might unleash upon us.

afrore (*adj.*) frozen stiff, solid with frost [dial., 1746]

See **forfrorn**

aglidder (*adj.*) of the ground: coated in a glittering, yet very slippery, layer of frost or ice [dial., 1837; < OE *glidder*, 'slippery']

A none-too-distant relative of *glide*, *glidder* has meant slippery since Old English times. Although its use appears to have dwindled over the years, the word was maintained in a handful of English regions before being recorded for posterity in the dialect dictionaries of the mid 1800s, often in the forms *aglidder* or *gliddery*. Confusion with the similar yet unrelated word *glitter* is possibly responsible for the later association of *aglidder* with a surface that is not only slippery, but glisteningly reflective too; in fact, some nineteenth-century dictionaries list *glidder* as a local name for a coating of enamel, hinting at just the kind of pure white frost this word is perhaps intended to describe.

blunk (*v.*) to snow only very lightly [dial., 1746; ? < ME *blenk*, 'glance']

Also found as to *blenk* or even to *blenky*, the word *blunk* is recorded in a handful of dialects from the far southwest corner of England. Although its origins are a mystery, in the sense of merely touching upon a surface for a moment it is perhaps in some way related to an earlier Middle English word, *blenk*, for a rapid glance or glimpse. Either way, when the winter snow sets in – but is mercifully not yet too heavy – then it can be said to be just *blunking*.

cat-ice (*n.*) ice from beneath which the water has receded [1884]

If pools dry up or floodwaters recede while the temperature remains low, then layers of ice can remain in place without any liquid water beneath them. A floating layer of ice like this has been known as *cat-ice* since the mid nineteenth century at least – the implication being that the layer is so fragile that a cat could safely walk across it, but nothing else could.

chibbly (*adj.*) crisp and crackly with frost [dial., 1884; ? < *chippy*, 'brittle, fragmented']

When frost-covered ground lightly cracks and crackles as you walk across it, it can be said to be *chibbly*. A word pinpointed specifically to the county of Worcestershire by the *English Dialect Dictionary*, it is perhaps related to the adjective *chippy*, in the sense of the frost breaking brittlely into icy chips and fragments.

clinkerbell (*n.*) **an icicle [1842; ? < *clink*, 'to make a ringing sound' + *bell*]**

Most definitely not to be confused with *clinkerballs* ('balls of dried dung or dirt in a sheep's wool', according to the *English Dialect Dictionary*), the *Oxford English Dictionary* connects *clinkerbell* to the verb to *clink*, meaning to chime metallically. Another possible explanation, however, is that this is a dialect alteration of a *clinger*, in reference to spikes of ice clinging resolutely to the eaves and overhangs of buildings.

clock-faces (*n.*) **thin discs of ice floating on the surface of a body of water [dial., 1864]**

Thin translucent circles of ice can often be seen floating on the surface of calm lakes, ponds and rivers in wintertime, but in colder regions and further out at sea these floating circles can become far larger and thicker, in which case they are known as *ice pancakes*. They are formed when the surface of a body of water begins to freeze, but the action of the water or waves causes the growing masses of ice to bump together, simultaneously rounding their edges while keeping them detached from one another.

clock-ice (*n.*) **ice that has cracked in straight lines out from a central point, like the hands of a clock [dial., 1854]**

Step on a frozen puddle whose ice is just thin enough to break, but still thick enough to hold together, and you may find a radiating network of cracks spread out across its surface from beneath your feet.

> *A term applied to ice much cracked in various fantastic, and sometimes even beautiful, forms. This phenomenon*

> *is frequently occasioned by pressure on the surface, as in skaiting* [sic] . . . *while the plate of ice is firmly attached to the shore or bank; and sometimes it arises from the variable temperature of the air, which, under certain conditions, is inclosed in the ice, producing contractions and expansions, and consequently those fantastic fissures.*
>
> Anne Elizabeth Baker, *A Glossary of Northamptonshire Words and Phrases* (1854)

conglaciate (*v.*) to freeze, to form or become ice [1646; < Lat. *con–*, 'together' + *glacies*, 'ice']

As well as simply meaning to freeze or turn into ice, *conglaciate* (which derives from the same Latin root as *glacier*) can also be used to mean to polish a surface to a smooth, glassy finish.

crazzled (*adj.*) only very slightly frozen or crisp with ice [dial., 1790; ? < *crazed*, 'broken up, covered in fine cracks']

A word from the dialects of Yorkshire in particular, *crazzled* is perhaps related to the adjective *crazed*, when used to describe the slightly broken and fragmented surface of a piece of pottery: before it came to be used of slightly frozen or frosty ground, *crazzled* was used of especially dry ground that had broken up into a fine network of cracks.

> *In a long drought, when the surface in the bog is dry and crazzled over, there is a scarcity of water in the wells.*
>
> Thomas Short, *A General Treatise on Various Cold Mineral Waters in England* (1765)

See also **chibbly**

creange (*v.*) **of ice or frozen ground, to crackle when broken or stepped upon [dial., 1892; ? < onomatopoeic]**

Not just linked to crackling ice, the verb *creange* can apparently be used of any brittle or fragile surface that breaks apart with a cracking sound as pressure is applied to it: 'To crackle, as thin ice does in breaking, or as woodwork when it is crushed' is how this was defined in an 1892 *Glossary of Words Used in the County of Northumberland*.

crump (*v.*) **to walk over crisp ground [1789; ? < onomatopoeic]**

A collection of oddly satisfying words including *crimp*, *crump* and *crumpy* have been used to describe anything crunchy or brittle since the mid 1500s. From there, the verb *crump* emerged roughly two centuries later, initially meaning 'to emit a crisp, crackling sound, as ice [or] snow . . . when trodden on', according to the *English Dialect Dictionary*, before extending to the act of walking across crisp or 'crumpy' ground itself.

See also **crumping**

feefle (*v.*) **of snow: to swirl or whirl in the wind [1958; Sc., ? < rel. Sc.** ***feef*****, 'a wisp, a puff of air']**

'To swirl, as of snow round a corner' is how the *Scottish National Dictionary* defines this one. *Feef* is an older Scots word for a short puff or blast of air, although whether or not that is related to this word is unclear; an alternative theory is that *feefle* is a figurative extension of an earlier Scots word, to *fiffle* or *fifle*, meaning to act foolishly or muddle-headedly, perhaps in the sense of the snow whirling wildly around.

flindrikin (*n.*) a light fall or dusting of snow [Sc., ? *c.* 1800; ? < Sc. *Flanderkin*, 'from Flanders']

Flindrikin has been in recorded use in Scots for at least 200 years, in a variety of senses all bearing some suggestion of flimsiness, frivolousness or unsubstantialness. As well as meaning a light-headed person, slight or flimsy material and even a very thin oatcake, its use in relation to a mere dusting of snow appears to have been a more recent development, found in print no earlier than the mid 1900s (though as always, an absence of written evidence does not necessarily mean a term was not in spoken use somewhat earlier). Etymologically, the word's origins are something of a mystery too, although at least one explanation suggests there may be some reference to especially fine Flanders lace somewhere in the mix here, while another connects the word – in the sense of something flighty and insubstantial – to *vlinder*, the Dutch for 'butterfly'.

forfrorn (*adj.*) frozen solid, trapped in ice [1481; < *for*– + *froren*, ME past tense of *freeze*]

Had the etymological meanderings of English gone the other way, today *froren* and *frore* rather than *froze* and *frozen* would be the past-tense forms of the verb *freeze*; all four were permissible in the Middle English period, but only the latter pair has stood the test of time. That being said, the older variants *froren* and *frore* survive in a handful of less used, long-forgotten and dialectal words and expressions, including **afrore** and this word, *forfrorn*.

The initial *for*– here is an intensifier, implying a sense of totality or completeness. Other supremely useful words that share the same root include long-lost gems like *forspent* (utterly used up), *forraked* (worn out by walking), *forwallowed* (exhausted from tossing and turning all night) and *forlaboured* (overworked) – all of which may well come in handy as the winter months pass by.

frostwork (*n.*) the geometric patterns formed on a surface by frost or ice [1631]

It can be difficult to appreciate how intricate a surface of ice actually is when it merely forms on the ground or across the surface of a puddle or pool of water. But when it forms on a windowpane or a car windscreen, for example, its complex geometry and radiating *frostwork* are often far more visible. That being said, it is still an endlessly frustrating nuisance when you're late for work and can't see to drive – but at least it's a pretty one.

flother (*n.*) a single flake of snow [13thC; ? < OE *flaðra*, snowflakes]

A Middle English word that has, regrettably, long since fallen by the linguistic wayside. The *fl–* pairing of sounds seems for many years to have implied some sense of lightly moving through the air or to the ground, thanks to its appearance in words like *fly*, *flap* and *flutter*. Similarly, as well as *flother*, a single snowflake has also been known over the centuries as a *flaw* (fourteenth century), a *flaught* (fifteenth century) and a *flaughen* (early nineteenth century).

frost-dogs (*n.*) tiny frozen particles of falling snow [dial., 19thC; *frost* + *dog* , cf. water-dog]

Snow is already frozen, of course, but *frost-dogs* are the minuscule glistening particles of snow that are so small and light that they often seem to hang in the air rather than fall to the ground. They 'can just be seen falling on a sunny winter's day', according to the *English Dialect Dictionary*.

glaur **(*n.*)** **a patch of slippery ice [dial., 1880; ? < *glare*]**

As a noun, the word *glare* has been used to mean iciness, or a fine coating of ice or frost, since the 1500s. *Glaur* is perhaps a local dialect alteration of that, recorded from the mid nineteenth century onwards as a word for an especially slippery patch of icy ground.

glottening **(*n.*)** **a partial thaw; a temporary melting of ice or snow [1847; < *glotten*, 'to thaw gently', of unknown origin]**

Glotten is a Scots and North Country word meaning to thaw slowly or gently. By the mid 1800s, it had found its way into a landmark *Dictionary of Archaic and Provincial Words*, where the addendum that this gentle thaw was only a temporary state of affairs was added into the mix. Quite where that particular extra detail came from – and, for that matter, where the word's earlier origins lie – are entirely unknown.

gourdness **(*n.*)** **of ice, a lack or want of slippiness [1825; ? < Fr. *gourd*, 'numb; inept']**

Likely adopted from French, the word *gourd* fell into use in English towards the end of the eighteenth century to describe anything that was stiff, immobile or difficult to wield or open. From there, it underwent a slightly imaginative twist in the early 1800s and began to be used of ice that is not as slippery as it might seem. Ultimately, should you ever be in a position to actively *want* ice to be more slippery than it is, *gourdness* is a rather puzzling wintry word for a lack or want of icy slickness.

greymin (*n.*) a very thin or meagre fall of snow [dial., 1805; < *griming* < *grime*, 'thin coating of dirt or grease']

Etymologically, this is literally a 'griming' of snow – that is, just a very thin layer suggestive of a fine coating of dirt or muck. According to one nineteenth-century definition, in fact, a *greymin* of snow is just sufficient to cover the ground or the roofs of buildings.

See also **grimet**

grimet (*adj.*) of the ground, covered in a mixture of patches of fresh snow and pools of meltwater [dial., 1905; ? < *grime*]

Probably a dialect extension of *grime* or *grimy* (in the same context as in **greymin**), a *grimet* was described in one early twentieth-century definition as descriptive of ground that is 'covered with a very thin layer of snow . . . with bare patches here and there, when a thaw has set in'.

hammelled (*adj.*) covered in frozen dew or moisture [dial., 1897; ? < OE *hamelian*, 'to damage, to maim']

In Old English, *hamelian* meant to maim or mutilate something, or to damage it in some manner in order to (often deliberately) render it useless. Over time, that morphed into the verb to *hamble*, or *hammel*, which has been used over the centuries to refer to all manner of similar gruesome practices, from docking tails to cutting hamstrings. Could such a bloodthirsty term really have given us a word for nothing more than frozen dew? Perhaps with reference to frostbitten plants or crops, there is a sense of being 'hambled' hiding behind this word – or perhaps, given the description of the related word **hemel** in the previous chapter, the implication is of roads or routes being rendered icily impassable.

hap (*n.*) a heavy, blanketing fall of snow [1891; < *hap*, 'to blanket']

As a verb, *hap* has been in use since medieval times to mean to wrap or densely cover something, both merely for warmth or protection (as if swaddling an infant) and in a more extreme sense (as if smothering or enfolding something entirely). By the 1500s, it had come to be used as a noun too, relating to any manner of thick blanket or insulating coverlet (while in the seventeenth century a *hip-hap* was a bustle-like adornment worn wrapped around the hips). And it is from there that in the mid nineteenth century the word eventually came to be used more figuratively of an all-covering layer of snow.

See also **hapwarm**

hogamadog (*n.*) a ball of snow made larger by rolling it through a snowfield [dial., 1892; < *hodmandod*, 'snail']

There is a rather complex chain of etymological connections running through this particular snowfield, covering somewhere in the region of 500 years.

Earliest of all, back in the mid 1500s or thereabouts, the word *dodman*, or *dodden*, emerged in a handful of English counties as a regional name for a snail. No one is entirely sure where that first came from, but by the seventeenth century it had been somewhat randomly and playfully extended into all manner of quirky regional nicknames, including *hoddy-dod*, *hodman-Hob*, *hoddamadod* and even *hoddymandoddy*. Then, in the late nineteenth century, a final word in this family, *hogamadog*, came to be used in the northern counties of England to refer to an ever-growing ball of rolled snow – the kind that might be used to start the body and head of a snowman. As for the somewhat puzzling connection between these two meanings? Well, it appears to be nothing more than the spiralling shape of a snail's shell, which is mirrored by the gradually growing snowball as it is rolled along the ground.

icelet (*n.*) an icicle; a drop of meltwater from the tip of an icicle [dial., 1883; lit. 'little piece of ice' < *ice* + *–let*]

In English *–let* is a diminutive-forming suffix, meaning that it can be used to form words bearing some sense of smallness, as in the likes of *leaflet*, *piglet* and *rivulet*. So an *icelet* is in effect just a 'little' mass or accumulation of ice – or, more especially, an icicle. The reference to a drop of meltwater from an icicle appears to be a later added detail, recorded in editions of the *Scottish National Dictionary* since the mid 1900s.

See also **meldrop**

icescape (*n.*) a wintry, ice-covered landscape [1839; < *ice* + *–scape*, < *landscape*]

The word *landscape* was borrowed into English from Dutch, *landschap*, in the early 1600s. Etymologically, the '–scape' at the end of *landscape* is the Dutch equivalent of the '–ship' at the end of words like *friendship* and *citizenship*, and is a distant relative of *shape*. Despite its curious origins, *landscape* quickly fell into use in English and became so familiarised that its *–scape* inspired a slew of other words for expanses or vistas, including this one – which can also be used in artistic contexts for a picture of a wintry landscape – from the early 1800s. A similar term, *winterscape*, followed in 1884, alongside other long-overlooked gems like *roofscape* (1891, a view over a city's rooftops), *nightscape* (1915, a nocturnal landscape) and *dunescape* (1928, a view of the desert or coastal sands).

See also **winterpiece**

laying-weather (*n.*) wintry conditions in which snow falls thickly enough to blanket the ground and remain in place for a long time [dial., 1840]

A term that apparently started out among the farmers of East Anglia.

lolly (*n.*) a slushy mixture of ice and snow floating on the surface of the water at a shoreline [Canada, 1792; < *loblolly*, 'gruel']

Loblolly is a sixteenth-century word for a thick but meagre gruel or stew (and in particular one served to sailors on board a ship) made from whatever remaining supplies a ship's cook has at their disposal. It was likely seafaring types who took this word across the Atlantic Ocean in the mid 1700s, where in the USA *loblolly* came to be used figuratively of a gloopy, slimy mud pool, while across the border in Canada a clipped form, *lolly*, came to refer to a slushy, miry mixture of snow and ice floating on the surface of the sea. It is, according to one nineteenth-century account, 'the hardest kind of thing to get the boat through' when approaching a shore or harbour.

moorkavie, murkavi (*n.*) a dense blinding storm, particularly one consisting of very fine snow [Sc., 1894; < *moor* + *kavie*, both meaning 'dense snowfall' < ON]

This curious word is made all the curiouser by being comprised of two separate roots – both of Scandinavian origin – that both independently mean a snowstorm. On its own, the word *moor* can be used in Scots to mean a dense fall of powdery snow, and is thought to have its roots in a Nordic term meaning something along the lines of a mass or swarm. *Kavie*, or *kaavie*, meanwhile, can likewise be used of a blizzard, or even a heavy rainstorm. It is related to *kafafjúk*, an Old Norse word for a thick fall of snow.

muldry (*adj.*) describing earth that has been broken up by the action of frost [dial., 1830; < *moulder*, 'to crumble']

If something *moulders*, then it decays or crumbles away to dust, and since the early 1600s the adjective *mouldery* has been used to describe soil that has done just that. In a handful of English dialects, however, a regionalised form of this word, *muldry*, emerged in the early nineteenth century to specifically describe earth that has been 'pulverised by frost', according to the *English Dialect Dictionary*.

murg (*n.*) a heavy, blanketing fall of snow; (*v.*) to trudge through snow [Sc., 1908; < Nor. dial. *morke*, 'clump']

Murg can be used to mean both a heavy, all-covering fall of snow and, as a verb, to trudge through a snowfield. Helpfully, the word has gained a figurative meaning too: in allusion to arduously slogging your way through deep snow, to *murg* can be used to mean to labour perseveringly through a raft of unpleasant work – which makes this a doubly useful word at this time of year, given all the pre-Christmas preparations going on.

Like a lot of words from the far north of Scotland, *murg* has its roots in Scandinavia and is thought to be related to an old Norwegian dialect word, *morke*, for a large shapeless mass or clump. From there, it is easy to see how this might have come to be used of a heavy fall of snow.

> *Murg, also morg . . . To work one's way painstakingly and perseveringly through a pile of work . . . to work constantly*

with a pile of unpleasant material, such as in cleaning fish, potatoes, etc.
Scottish National Dictionary

ninguid (*adj.*) covered in snow [1656; < Lat. *ninguis*, 'snow']

A snow-covered landscape is a *ninguid* landscape. That's a seventeenth-century term derived directly from a Latin word for snow, *ninguis*, that in its plural form, *ningues*, meant snowdrifts.

old-fashioned (*adj.*) of a winter: bringing heavy snow and thick frost [1829]

Given our warming climate today, it might be tempting to think that labelling a winter marked by thick snow and frost as 'old-fashioned' must be a modern turn of phrase. In fact, this two-centuries-old term was likely coined in retrospective reference to what we now know as the Little Ice Age – a period of intensely cold weather, from the sixteenth to nineteenth centuries, during which temperatures plunged across much of the North Atlantic region.

Quite what caused this 400-year winter lull has been subject to scientific debate ever since the Ice Age was first identified several decades ago, with everything from shifting ocean currents to increasing volcanic activity said to be to blame. The people who first used this term in the 1820s to look back on the old-fashioned winters of the previous century (through somewhat frost-tinted glasses) did not have long to wait for them to return, however: the Little Ice Age had a sting in its tail, and a final noticeable spell of cold weather and hard winters struck around 1850, and lasted until the turn of the new century.

pipkrake (*n.*) a single strand or crystal of needle ice; needle ice itself [1936; < Sw. *pip*, 'tube' + *krake*, 'thin, weak']

Needle ice is a curious winter weather phenomenon in which feathery, elongated strands of groundwater ice produce delicate clumps of tiny frozen pillars on the ground. It forms only when the temperature of the soil is above 0°C, but the temperature of the overlying air is below 0°C. The difference between the two causes moisture to be drawn out of the soil by capillary action and then to freeze on contact with the cold air above it. As ever more of this moisture is drawn upwards, the ice begins to build up on itself, forming a tiny needle-thin strand, often barely an inch or two in length. Each of these individual strands is known as a *pipkrake*, a term adopted into English from Swedish in the early 1900s, and derived in part from the Swedish word for a pipe or tube. The term can also be used more generally of needle ice itself – which, in rather less glamorous terms, can likewise be called **spew frost**, in allusion to the ice being 'thrown up' from the ground.

pruinescence (*n.*) frostiness; the quality of being covered in frost or ice [1890; < Lat. *pruina*, 'hoar frost']

Pruina was a Latin word for a thick frost or hoar, and is the origin of a clutch of similar words including *pruinose* (a botanical term describing leaves or fruits, like blueberries, that often have a frosty, powdery surface), *pruinous* (coated in frost) and *pruinescence* (frostiness, or the quality of being frost-covered).

punder (*v.*) the blowing of loose snow from the top or surface of something by the wind [dial., 1888; of unknown origin, ? rel. *pound*]

'To be blown or whiffed away by the wind' is how at least one nineteenth-century dictionary explained this old Yorkshire dialect word, which seems more often than not to have been used in relation to wisps of loose snow being blown across open moorland and hilltops.

> *'I were goin' on t'moor side, and t'snow were punderin' off o' t' top.' This was said when the wind was blowing snow off the hill in a fine powder.*
>
> Sidney Oldall Addy, *A Glossary of Words Used in the Neighbourhood of Sheffield* (1888)

rone (*n.*) a sheet of ice formed by melting snow freezing solid in cold weather, especially one used by children to slide upon [Sc., 1535; ? < *rone*, 'gutter']

The origin of this word is something of a mystery, not helped by the fact that innumerable variations of it (*roan*, *rhone*, *ronnie*, *rowin*) have been recorded over the past five centuries or so. One theory suggests that it is related to an identical word, *rone*, for a gutter or manmade channel for carrying off rainwater, the origins of which are thought to lie in Scandinavia. That being said, however, the most plausible explanation here may in fact be the simplest: given the added detail that children often used to slide along the *rone*, perhaps this is somehow descended from the word *run*.

scowthery (*adj.*) threatening to or just beginning to rain or snow [Sc., 1923; of unknown origin]

Scowther, or *scowder*, is a curious and wide-ranging eighteenth-century word that first meant to singe or just to catch slightly in the heat of a fire. From there, it picked up a huge variety of meanings and senses over the decades that followed, all bearing some suggestion of the slightest hint, touch or threat of something – among them a jellyfish sting, a frostbitten patch of discoloration on a plant, a child's chastisement and a fleeting feeling of disappointment or chagrin. By the mid 1800s, the word had also come to be used of a passing shower of rain or snow, before – in an even more fleeting or immaterial sense – it at long last inspired an adjective, *scowthery*, describing the appearance of a sky that seems to threaten bad or wintry weather to come.

shoggle, shuggle (*n.*) a noticeably large piece of ice floating down a river [1825; < *ice-shoggle*, 'icicle']

It is by no means unusual for words to change shape as they are passed down the centuries, but the chain of developments that ended up at *shoggle* must rank among the most convoluted.

Back in the Old English period, an icicle was a *gicle*. *Ice* was later attached to that to give us the bones of the word as it has become today, but in the melting pot of regional variation and outside influences that was medieval England, it was not long before that word began to morph into all manner of strange variant forms, and it continued to change shape over the centuries that followed. By the 1700s, *icicle* had turned into *ice-sickle*, then *ice-shockle* and finally *ice-shoggle*, before that was at long last clipped down to *shoggle*.

Given that the original word, *icicle*, had survived intact all this time, however, *shoggle* was somewhat surplus to requirements. So as a result it picked up a distinct meaning of its own, and by the early 1800s had come to be used of 'a large piece of ice floating down a river, after the ice is broken up', according to one 1825 explanation.

shot-ice (*n.*) the flat, thin expanses of ice that form on the surfaces of roads and pavements [1868; ? < *sheet*, 'expanse of ice']

Nothing to do with your feet 'shooting' out from under you should you happen to step on it, the 'shot' in *shot-ice* is actually thought to be nothing more than an alteration of *sheet*.

silver-thaw (*n.*) a shimmering coating of ice or frost, formed by freezing rain or melted snow [1770]

Also known as **verglas**, a silver-thaw is caused by rain or melting snow almost immediately freezing again, creating a glistening coating of glass-like ice. It may look beautiful in a seasonal **ice-scape**, but the moisture locked up in silver-thaw is far heavier than it looks, and in stormy conditions can weigh down and even break off large branches and boughs from ice-covered trees.

skiffer (*v.*) to rain or snow only very gently [dial., 1880; < skiff, 'to bounce']

To *skiffer* or *skifter* is an extended form of the older verb *skiff*, which has been used since the 1700s to mean to bounce or skim quickly and lightly across the surface of something.

slushpan (*n.*) a pool of melted snow [1876; < *slush* + *pan*, 'hole, recess in the ground']

'A snow-hole containing thawed or muddy contents' is how one nineteenth-century dictionary defined this word, while another labelled it 'a pool of melted snow or liquid mud in a road or on a moor'.

snarry (*adj.*) piercingly, bitingly cold [dial., late 19thC; < *snar*, 'ill-humoured']

Someone described as *snar* or *snaur* is surly and bad tempered, and so by extension winter weather that is similarly hostile and unpleasant can be described using the Yorkshire dialect word *snarry*.

snaw-rink (*n.*) a snow-covered road; a slippery, partially frozen patch of snow [Sc., 1877; < Sc. *snaw*, 'snow' + *rink*, 'expanse of ice']

In the sense of an area for skating or winter sports, *rink* comes from an Old French word, *renc*, for a space set aside for jousting or battle practice. Despite its familiarity today, the word remained largely confined to Scottish literature until as recently as the nineteenth century (meaning the first sport it was used in relation to was curling, not hockey or skating), and for a long time was used in Scots for any wide open space, regardless of its surface. A *snaw-rink*, ultimately, is a snow-covered 'rink' in this older, rather more general sense than we are used to today.

snow-bench (*n.*) a thick mass or bank of snow-filled clouds [1904; < *snow* + *bench*, 'long mass of cloud']

In particular, this refers to a long bench-like mass of cloud covering the far horizon, which is said to portend a heavy fall of snow.

snow-blossom (*n.*) a snowflake [1676]

Oddly, this word actually predates *snowflake* in writing by more than sixty years.

spew frost (*n.*) needle ice [1938; *spew*, 'something ejected upwards' + *frost*]

See **pipkrake**

spicula (*n.*) a single needle-like projection of ice or frost [1783; < Lat. *spiculum*, 'spike, sharp point']

As well as meaning a single spine of ice, over the centuries the word *spicula* has variously been applied to an animal's prickle, a plant's thorn and any sharp-pointed fragment or shard. Appropriately enough, it literally means 'little spike' in Latin.

stepmother's breath (*n.*) a sudden cold snap; a freezing gust of wind [1765]

It is not just in fairy tales that stepmothers have a bad reputation, but in the weather too. The long-standing stereotype of stepmothers being cruel and unfriendly is the origin of this eighteenth-century expression for a sudden period of cold weather or a bitingly cold blast of wind.

subnivean (*adj.*) lying beneath a covering of snow [1845; < Lat. *sub–*, 'beneath' + *niveus*, 'snowy' (< *nix*, 'snow')]

Derived from another Latin word for snow, *subnivean* is one of a number of locational adjectives referring to wintry landscapes, alongside *transnivean* ('located beyond the snows'), *subnival* ('living beneath the snow') and *cisnivean* ('found on this side of the snows', a word once especially used in reference to the Himalayas).

See also **subnivium**

subnivium (*n.*) the winter ecosystem found beneath the snow [?21stC; *sub–*, 'beneath' + *nivium*, Lat. 'of the snows' (< *nix*, 'snow')]

Go for a walk in the country on a cold winter's day and the snowy world around you may seem somewhat barren and lifeless. With lakes iced over, no leaves on the trees and many birds having long ago returned to their wintering grounds, a winter habitat can feel like little more than a white desert. But looks can be deceiving, as beneath the snow lies the *subnivium* – a lively winter ecosystem, trapped between a thick covering of snow and the ground below it.

As well as plants and flowers seeing out the winter in suspended animation, the subnivium is home to a host of smaller creatures, like mice and voles, that use the overlying snow cover both as a kind of insulation, shielding them from the colder air above, and as a security measure, protecting them from predators. Heat both from the ground and from what little sunshine there may be at this time of year often causes the snowpack covering the subnivium to melt partly too, and as its snow crystals shift and expand, these tiny creatures are able to utilise the gaps that movement frees up to dig out vast networks of concealed tunnels. There may not appear to be much going on from our vantage point, but out of sight things are seemingly just as busy as the rest of the year.

See also **subnivean**

theeking (*v.*, *adj.*) of a fall of snow: thick enough to pile up on the roofs of houses [1846; < ME *theek*, 'thatch']

Theek or *theck* was a Middle English variant of the same word that would later give us our *thatched* rooftops, and it is in the sense of a thick layer covering the top of a building that this delightfully precise word emerged in the nineteenth century.

A 'theaking snow' quietly but continuously falling, so as to cover thickly, as thatch does, a house.

J. T. & W. E. Brockett, *A Glossary of North Country Words* (1846)

twanking (*adj.*) of frost or cold: keenly biting [dial., 1873; ? < *twank*, 'to beat']

To *twank* is to beat or thrash soundly, and it is possible that the bizarre word *twanking* uses that root somewhat figuratively to describe a similarly harsh and brutal frost. Alternatively, in the sense of something especially potent or powerful, there might be a link here to an old northern English dialect word, *twanker*, for anything or anyone noticeably sizeable. Just be very careful how you use all three of those in polite conversation.

verglas (*n.*) a coating of ice or frost, formed by freezing rain [1808; < Fr., lit. 'glass ice']

See **silver-thaw**

wap, whap (*n.*) a sudden heavy snowstorm [1818; < ME *whapp*, 'heavy blow']

Despite appearances, this word was probably once onomatopoeic and appears to have been invented in the Middle English period to represent the sound of a stout knock or blow. On that basis, it has long since amassed a number of alternative meanings, all bearing some sense of an unexpected attack or disturbance, of which this sudden snowstorm is just one. Elsewhere, a *wap* can be a brawl or wrestling match, a noisy quarrel, a strong gust of wind or, according to the *Scottish National Dictionary*, 'a drinking bout conjoined with noise and confusion'.

windcrust (*n.*) a toughened, partially frozen crust of snow formed by cold winds [1936]

An expanse of snow can sometimes form a noticeable crust on top of it due to the action of weak sunlight, which melts only the very topmost layer before it promptly refreezes. When conditions are just right, however, the movement of ice-cold air over a snowfield can have much the same effect, producing a thin and slightly toughened upper layer of snow that cracks and splinters when walked or skied across – or in other words, a *windcrust*.

yertdrift (*n.*) snow blown up into drifts from the ground [Sc. (Orkney), 1929; < Sc. *yert*, 'earth' + *drift*]

yowdendrift (*n.*) drifting snow driven rapidly downwards from the sky by strong winds [Sc., 1790; ? < Sc. *yowden*, 'yield' + *drift*]

Both of these words clearly have similar meanings, and as a result are often given definitions making them out to be all but interchangeable. There does seem to have been a difference between them at some point in time at least, however, namely that a *yertdrift* is formed by snow that is already on the ground being blown up into drifts, while a *yowdendrift* is formed by snow being driven forcefully down from the heavens by strong winds.

Yert, in this context, is just a Scots word for 'earth' (in the sense of the snow becoming piled up on the ground), but *yowden* is far trickier to account for. One popular theory claims that it is somehow related to the word *yield* (of which *yowden* was once an obscure past-tense form), but perhaps a more likely explanation is that it is connected to an equally obscure verb, *youden*, meaning to move or agitate.

zneesy (*adj.*) cold, frosty [sl., 1725; ? < *sneeze*]

In eighteenth-century slang, *znees* was frost, so if the weather was *zneesy* then it was cold and icy. Straightforwardly enough, it seems likely that both words are no more than playfully slangy alterations of *sneeze* – just the kind of thing that might result from such weather.

4. KEEPING COSY

Although the winter weather can be decidedly unpleasant, at the same time there is something appealing about layering on your thickest clothing and seeing out the worst of the snow, wind and rain from the blissful comfort of somewhere warm. In fact, the winter months give us more than ample opportunity to wrap up snugly and make a cosy refuge for ourselves, perhaps by the fireside at home or in a comfortable country pub with a welcome glass of something warming in our hands. From **antifogmatic** drinks to body-warming bouts of **slappaty-pouch**, the words in this chapter are all about keeping the cold at bay.

antifogmatic (*n.*) a drink taken to combat the effects of cold or damp weather [US sl., 1789; < *anti–*, 'against' + *fog* + *–matic* (? < *rheumatic*, or *automatic*)]

A warming drink taken on a cold winter's day can also be known as a *fog-breaker* or *fog-cutter*, but an *antifogmatic* – a name apparently intended to sound like that of a medicinal preparation – is the earliest such invention. Recorded in the USA at the tail end of the eighteenth century, the word was first applied to a warming glass of rum.

bronse (*v.*) to make oneself too warm by sitting too close or too long by a fire [Sc., 1808; ? < *bronze*]

To *bronse* can also be used of the act of overheating by sitting in the sun too long (though that's perhaps less of a concern at this time of year).

calefactory (*n.*) something or somewhere that warms [1536; < Lat. *calor*, 'heat']

Derived from the same Latin root as *calorie*, *calefactory* has had a handful of rather niche meanings over the centuries, including a metal pan used to heat the hands of a priest about to deliver the Eucharist, and a communal room in a monastery where monks could go to keep warm. The more general sense of anything or anywhere that provides heat emerged in the seventeenth century, so that today the word could effectively be applied to anything from a hot cup of tea to a cosy fireside **sonrock**.

chimonophile (*n.*) a lover of wintry weather [? 19thC; < Gk. *cheimon*, 'winter' + *–phile* (< Gk. *philos*, 'beloved, loving')]

Not everyone thinks the winter months are unpleasant, of course, and a fondness for wintry weather is known as *chimonophilia*. Someone who exhibits precisely that is therefore a *chimonophile* – and happily the same word applies even if your idea of enjoying the winter is through a window while sat cosily indoors.

See also ***gluggaveður***

coldrife (*adj.*) easily chilled, prone to feeling the cold [1773; < *cold* + *rife*, 'commonplace, widespread']

Coldrife is a word particularly in use in Scots, with the '–rife' ending here being the same *rife* we use when something is especially prevalent or abounding. As well as being *coldrife* (that is, essentially 'abounding with coldness'), you can also be *wakerife* (*c.* 1500, unable to sleep), *coolrife* (1768, indifferent), *sickrife* (1808, slightly unwell or prone to illness), *mockrife* (1818, scornful) and *wastrife* (1818, recklessly spendthrift).

cotlight (*n.*) light seen shining warmly through the window of a house from outside [dial., 1796; < *cot*, 'small dwelling' + *light*]

A *cot* is a small cottage or dwelling-place, which makes *cotlight* the cosy and cheering glow of a light shining through the windows of a welcoming building – the perfect sight after a long winter's walk or journey.

> *See! though night comes, dark and eerie,*
> *Yon sma' cot-light cheers the dale!*
>
> Hector Macneill, 'The Waes o' War' (1796)

croodle, crowdle (*v.*) to huddle or sit close together for warmth [dial., 1788; of unknown origin, ? < *crowd*]

Recorded in a host of dialects across Britain and Ireland, *croodle* is a word as delightful to say as it is to do on a cold winter's day.

> *To CROWDLE (diminutive of crowd); to creep close together, as children round the fire, or chickens under the hen.*
>
> William Marshall, *Provincialisms of East Yorkshire* (1788)

crule (*v.*) to move closer to the fire when cold [1775; ? < *crawl*]

Likely derived from *crawl*, to *crule* is specifically 'to draw near the fire shivering as though cramped with cold', according to one eighteenth-century definition.

fire-scordel (*n.*) someone – and in particular, a house cat – who sits happily by the fire all day [dial., 1886; ? < dial. *scroodle*, 'crouch']

Scordel is a Devonshire form of the old verb *scroodle*, meaning to cower or crouch, so a *fire-scordel* is someone who would very happily spend an entire winter's day crouched or 'scroodled' by the fire – or, according to one source at least, a cat that likes to do just that:

> *A domestic servant, a native and resident of Ashburton* [in Devon], *said, 'Our cat is a regular fire-scordel.' When asked the meaning, she said, 'A fire cat, or ash cat,' that, 'scordels over the fire.'*
>
> Alfred Gregory, *Devonshire Verbal Provincialisms* (1886)

See also **vire-spannel**

froust, frowst (*n.*) extra time in bed on Sundays; (*v.*) to keep warm, or take pleasure from keeping warm [19thC sl., 1880; ? < *frowsty*, 'stuffy']

A noun and a verb that will not only keep you cosy in cold weather, but also let you make the most of doing so on a chilly weekend. The word *frowsty* has been in use for 200 years or so to describe somewhere stuffy and fusty, like the air inside a long unopened room. In the late 1800s, that word apparently inspired a noun, *frowst*, which first proved popular among boarding-school children to describe the extra time they were permitted to stay in bed on Sundays (the implication presumably being that festering in a warm bed long after you might otherwise be up is liable to produce a 'frowsty' atmosphere under the covers). Lastly, towards the end of the nineteenth century, a verb *frowst* emerged in a similar context, meaning to happily keep oneself warm in cold weather.

> *It is men and women who are growing colder, not the year. A generation that frousts over the fire, that is flannelled up to the chin, and swathed down to the ankles, that shuts out from its houses every breath of fresh air.*
>
> 'Our Mode of Life', *The Homoeopathic World* (1884)

gluggaveður **(*n.*) weather that looks nice from indoors, but you would not want to be outside in it [Icel., lit. 'window weather']**

Given that temperatures struggle to make the mid-teens even at the height of summer there, it is perhaps unsurprising that Iceland has a rather well-furnished vocabulary of winter words. *Mjöll*, for instance, is freshly fallen snow in Icelandic, while *lausamjöll* is especially loose snow, *bleytuslag* is wet deep snow, *slydda* is snow that is so wet and sleety that it might as well be raining, and *hundslappadrífa* ('snowflakes as large as the paws of dogs') is the serene, picture-perfect snowfall in which large fluffy snowflakes fall windlessly straight to the ground. Alongside all of those is the excellent Icelandic word *gluggaveður*, which is used of the kind of weather that is nice to look at, but only from the cosy comfort of the indoors. Appropriately enough, it literally translates as 'window weather'.

hapwarm (*n.*) a heavy, all-covering item of clothing worn in cold weather [Sc., dial., 1773; < hap]

You can't keep yourself cosy without the right clothes; case in point, the existence of the word **peel**. To *hap* is to cover or enwrap something warmly, which makes a *hapwarm* an insulating garment or coverlet that does precisely that.

See also **hap**

hibernaculum (*n.*) a winter refuge, somewhere to retreat to during the winter months [1699; < Lat. 'winter refuge' (< *hibernus*, 'winter')]

If your idea of seeing out the winter involves getting as far away from it as possible, then perhaps what you're after is a hibernaculum. Variously used over the centuries of a group of soldiers' wintertime quarters, the lair of a hibernating animal and even a greenhouse for wintering plants, the word *hibernaculum* comes from *hibernus*, a Latin word for winter.

hiemate (*v.*) to spend the winter somewhere [1623; < Lat. *hiems*, 'winter']

Like a less slumbersome version of hibernating, *hiemating* is the act of spending the winter months somewhere – not necessarily at home, and not necessarily asleep. So if your **hibernaculum** is not just a cosy refuge but, say, a tropical beach as far away from the elements as possible, then perhaps this is the optimal winter word for you.

See also **brumation, snowbird**

howffy (*adj.*) of a place: cosy and comfortable [Sc., dial., 1808; < *howf*, 'a familiar place']

A *howff* is a familiar haunt or meeting place – perhaps especially 'a much-frequented tavern', according to the *English Dialect Dictionary*. A warm country pub might be just what the doctor ordered when it comes to keeping cosy in winter, but in truth anywhere would be suitable so long as it feels *howffy* – that is, warm, snug and as familiarly comfortable as somewhere you know well.

kleptothermy (*n.*) a method of keeping warm in which one organism steals heat from another [1958; < *klepto–* (< Gk. *klepto*, 'steal') + *–thermy* (< Gk. *thermos*, 'heat']

This being a fairly formal biological term from the none-too-romantic field of thermoregulation, *kleptothermy* is hardly the cosiest-sounding of words or definitions. But if you're the kind of **coldrife** person who likes to snuggle in against someone else to keep yourself warm, then strictly speaking you're a *kleptotherm* – literally, a 'heat-thief'.

leep (*v.*) to relax or nestle together in a warm, cosy place [Sc., dial., 1866; < Sc. *leep*, 'to boil, to heat']

First used back in the sixteenth century to mean to boil or scald, the word *leep* amassed all manner of meanings and senses over the years, all relating to some form of cooking, heating, steeping or warming. By the 1800s, its meaning had drifted from the stovetop to the hearthside, with a handful of turn-of-the-century dictionaries variously defining it as 'to sit in a lazy manner over the fire', 'to be fond of warmth' or 'to snuggle up in some warm place'.

moble (*v.*) to dress in multiple layers of clothing to keep warm [? 17thC; of unknown origin]

When you find yourself wearing a hat, coat, gloves, scarf and boots on top of a jumper, shirt, trousers, thermals and at least two pairs of socks, then you can count yourself thoroughly *mobled*. This is a word of unclear but no less impressive heritage, with even Shakespeare writing of 'the mobled queen' in Act 2 of *Hamlet*. His version of the word seems to have meant veiled or muffled, rather than merely dressed for warmth, and it would be another two centuries before *mobled* was used explicitly in reference to insulating clothes: 'to put on an abundance of warm wraps . . . as when setting out for a cold journey or such like' is how one dictionary defined it back in 1879.

mufflements (*n. pl.*) thick, warm, insulating overclothes [dial., 1869; < *muffle* + *–ment*, suffix forming nouns from verbs]

When you're thoroughly **mobled**, it seems, you're wearing your *mufflements*. *Muffle* is a word from the Middle English period, thought to come from an equally ancient French word, *moufle*, for a fur mitten.

ombrifuge (*n.*) a shelter against the rain [1869; < *ombro–* (< Gk. *ombros*, 'rain shower') + *–fuge* (< Lat. *fugare*, 'to chase away, to drive off')]

paragrandine (*n.*) a device for protecting something against hail [1842; < *para–* (< Lat. *parare*, 'to prepare, to make ready') + Lat. *grando*, 'hail']

Keeping warm and cosy in the wintertime isn't just about sitting by a fire imbibing an **antifogmatic**, of course. If you get caught out by the changeable weather at this time of year, then you may well need to seek shelter outdoors – or, in more impressive terms, find an *ombrifuge* if it's raining, and a *paragrandine* if a hailstorm blows in.

***peiskos* (*n.*) the feeling of snug contentment or cosiness that comes from sitting by a warm indoor fireside [Nor., < *peis*, 'fireplace' + *kos*, 'cosiness']**

The Danish word *hygge* has proved something of a sensation in recent years, but its Norwegian cousin *peiskos* perhaps deserves just as much attention. The perfect word for leaving the cold outside and making the most of the warm indoors, it literally means 'fireside cosiness'.

pokertalk (*n.*) **casual fireside chatter [1885]**

When you're sitting with your **jamb-friends**, you'll doubtless be engaged in some *pokertalk* while gathered round the poker and tongs and other equipment kept at a fireside.

prinkling (*n., v.*) **the tingling sensation felt in cold extremities as they warm up [*c.* 1720; < *prinkle*, 'to tingle']**

As well as meaning to prickle like pins and needles, to *prinkle* can also mean to sparkle, to bubble like boiling water or to feel a shivering thrill on being touched. In relation to cold weather in particular, however, it can be used of the dull tingling feeling as fingers benumbed by the wintry conditions start to warm up as they're wrapped around a hot mug of tea.

rozzle (*v.*) **to bask or warm oneself in the heat of a fire [dial., 1827; ? < ME *rostle*, 'to burn']**

Rozzle is apparently descended from a medieval word, *rostle*, meaning to scorch or singe (which in turn likely comes from the same Old English root as *roast*). In some English dialects, *rozzle* also seems to have been used as a noun for the flushed, warming sensation of taking a gulp of strong liquor.

shawm (*v.*) **to warm your legs by the fire [Sc., dial., 1866; of unknown origin, ? < Sc. *scam*, 'scorch']**

'To warm oneself by thrusting the lower portion of the body close to the fire' is the *English Dialect Dictionary*'s definition of this peculiar word – but other definitions suggest an added implication of doing so when you really ought to be doing something else. An 1866 *Dialect of Banffshire*, for instance, defined the related adjective *shaumin'* as 'indolent, with the notion of sitting by the fire'. Keeping yourself cosy, it seems, is just too tempting.

sonrock (*n.*) a soft, cosy fireside chair [Ir., 1905; ? < *sunk*, 'soft chair']

This excellent yet decidedly mysterious word's origins are a complete unknown, but there is perhaps some kind of connection to an eighteenth-century word, *sunk* or *sonk*, for a chair – or, more specifically, a soft straw-filled pad often used to cushion a saddle.

snerdle (*v.*) to nestle comfortably together; to wrap up cosily in bed [dial., 1905; of unknown origin]

Like **croodle** before it, this is a word that sounds almost as appealing as its meaning. A dialect term pinpointed to the county of Nottinghamshire, *snerdling* can also apparently be used of slipping warmly and comfortably into a good, sound sleep.

sunnybank (*n.*) a fine warm fire in the wintertime [*c.* 1698; < *sunny*, in the sense of providing warmth + *bank*, ? 'mound of combustible material']

A slang term first used among eighteenth-century criminals, *sunnybank* was recorded in a handful of glossaries of slang right through to the late 1800s before falling out of use. 'A good rousing winter fire' is how a *Dictionary of the Canting Crew* defined this back in the 1690s.

thermogenesis (*n.*) the production of body heat [1891; < *thermo–* (< Gk. *thermos*, 'heat') + *–genesis* (< Gk. *genesis*, 'origin, beginning')]

thermolysis (*n.*) the loss of body heat [1896; < *thermo–* (< Gk. *thermos*, 'heat') + Gk. *lysis*, 'releasing, loosing']

The loss of body heat is called *thermolysis*, while the aim of the game when out and about in winter is *thermogenesis*. Anything that stimulates the production of body heat meanwhile – such as donning more **mufflements**, or a quick round of **slappaty-pouch** – can be described using the adjective *thermoexcitatory*.

thermophagy (*n.*) the craving or consumption of hot food [1860; < *thermo–* (< Gk. *thermos*, 'heat') + *–phagy* (< Gk. *phagein*, 'to eat']

thermoposia (*n.*) the consumption of hot drinks [1726; < *thermo–* (< Gk. *thermos*, 'heat') + Gk. *posis*, 'drinking']

thermolusia (*n.*) the taking of a warm bath [1868; < *thermo–* (< Gk. *thermos*, 'heat') + Gk. *lousis*, 'bathing']

All three of these terms were first employed in medical contexts, with the first used in relation to conditions that limited a patient's ability to perceive extremes of temperature; the second in the supposed treatment of scurvy by drinking large amounts of hot water; and the third describing the therapeutic use of warm baths to relieve aches, pains and the discomfort of various ailments. Even without any underlying issues, though, there are few things more restorative than a hot drink, a warm meal or a lazy soak in the tub in cold winter weather.

uneave (*v.*) to remove the chill or ice from something artificially, as by dowsing it with hot water [dial., 1891; ? < *heave*, 'move with effort']

Various forms of this word have been recorded over the decades in the dialects of southwest England, most especially in Devon and Cornwall. Given that some records spell it *unheave,* rather than *uneave,* perhaps the original implication here was of thawing something that has become locked stiff with cold, so that it can move and 'heave' into action once more.

vire-spannel (*n.*) a dog that likes to lie by the fire [dial., 1886; < lit. 'fire spaniel']

The canine equivalent of a **fire-scordel** is a *vire-spannel,* or literally a 'fire spaniel', according to an 1886 *Dictionary of the Isle of Wight Dialect.*

yule-clog (*n.*) an especially large log placed on a fire on Christmas Eve, intended to continue burning throughout the Christmas period [1834; < *yule* + *clog*, 'log']

The *clog* here is the same as the wooden shoe: a term dating back to the 1300s for a large, solid lump of wood. According to folklore, if the yule-clog is extinguished or burns out before Christmas ends, the household will endure bad luck in the coming year; selflessly using the flame from your fire to relight another household's yule-clog, moreover, risks forfeiting all your good fortune to them, and leaving you with twelve months of bad luck instead.

5. OUT IN THE ELEMENTS

Given the coldness and darkness of the winter months, chances are many of us would much rather stay indoors most of the time. But with going to work every day, walking the dog, taking the kids to school and picking up the groceries, leaving your cosy **hibernaculum** seems all but inevitable. Not to worry: this next set of words is dedicated to anything and everything you might need or encounter while you're out in the winter elements.

barflog (*v.*) to slap the arms crosswise against the chest and shoulders to keep warm [Sc., 1908; < ON *berja*, 'to beat']

Like **mirkabrod**, this is a word whose origins lie in Norn, the Nordic language once spoken in Shetland and Orkney. Thanks to those Scandinavian roots, *barflog* is thought to be related to an Old Norse word, *berja*, meaning to beat or strike forcefully. (A word of warning for this one, though: do not under any circumstances look this word up in the online Urban Dictionary.)

See also **cuff, slappaty-pouch**

bendy-leather (*n.*) a frozen coating or surface of ice over a puddle or pool of water that is slightly flexible, but does not give way when walked across [Sc., dial., 1898; < *bend*, *bend-leather*, a kind of strong, half-tanned oxhide used to make shoes]

Bendy-leather was apparently a term once widely used across southern Scotland and the northern counties of England by children playfully sliding or skating across patches of weak ice. Despite the apparent danger of the ice breaking, or the child slipping over and injuring themselves, there was at least a reassuring rhyme to go with the game: 'Bendy-leather's good to bear / Take a heart and never fear.'

bicker (*v.*) to pelt with snowballs [dial., *c.* 1828; ? < *bicker*, 'to brawl, to come to blows']

Nowadays we might be more inclined to use it to mean just to argue or bandy words, but when *bicker* first appeared in the language around the early fourteenth century, it meant to come to physical blows. At least part of that more hands-on definition survived down into the 1800s, when *bickering* could be used to describe striking with repeated blows or knocks – or, rather more playfully, to pelt repeatedly with snowballs.

break the brod, to (*v. phr.*) to be the first person to walk across a field of fresh snow [Sc., 1914; < Sc. *brod*, 'open road']

Wake up early enough, or take yourself off somewhere remote enough, and you may find an untouched snowfield in which to *break the brod*. An expression likely dating back to the 1800s, if not earlier, at its heart is the Scots word *brod*, or *bruid*, meaning an open road or clear pathway.

See also **feetings**

bulver (*v.*) to increase in bulk by being rolled over and over, like a snowball [1895; of unknown origin]

The definition above comes from an 1895 guide to the dialect of East Anglia – which, in the sense of a large, dense, ever-growing mass, also rather helpfully defines a *bulverhead* as 'one whose brains are a thick confused mass'.

See also **hogamadog**

chun (*n.*) a painful crack in the skin of the hands caused by cold weather [dial., 1877; of unknown origin, ? < *chine*, 'cleft, gap']

Fail to **moble** yourself sufficiently in your **mufflements** (or in simple terms, forget to bring your gloves when you head outside in wintertime) and the skin on your hands is often the first casualty. According to the *English Dialect Dictionary*, one of the painful cracks or fissures that can open up on the exposed skin of the hands in the cold is known as a *chun*, though quite where that word comes from is a mystery. Old English had a similar word, *cine*, for a crack or cleft in a surface, however, so perhaps *chun* could be somehow related to that. Or it might be a lone relic from the very earliest days of our language.

clart (*n.*) a single snowflake, large enough to stick to your clothes [dial., 1828; < *clart*, 'mess, dirt']

Clart is a word common to a host of English dialects, almost always in some sense of dirtiness, muddiness or messiness; among its multitude of other definitions are slime or sludge, a slovenly person, a dense mass of bread dough, and even sheep's wool matted with dung. The definition given here was first outlined in a dialect guide to West Yorkshire in the 1820s.

See also **flother, snow-blossom**

clumse (*adj.*) benumbed with cold [1611; < ME *clumsen*, 'to become numb']

As well as being an adjective, *clumse* can also be used as a verb meaning to become numb with cold – or more figuratively, to stupefy or strike someone dumb.

crumping (*n.*, *v.*) the light crunching sound of walking on thick or slightly frozen snow [1789; < onomatopoeic]

Everyone knows the curious rubbing sound made by walking through thick snow, and now you have the word to go with it. Like a lot of words in this vein, it was probably originally coined onomatopoeically, to mimic the sound of the shifting and crushing snow itself.

The shorten'd day shuts in,
An' fogs, condensing in the gelid air,
Upo' the plains fall hoary – Humid even'
Along the western sky its vapors trails
In chilly train; an' to the pliant foot
O' plodding passenger, the grassy path
Crumps sonorous.

David Davidson, 'Thoughts on the Seasons' (1789)

See also **crump**

cryophile (*n.*) something or someone that thrives in wintry conditions [1907; < *cryo–* (< Gk. *cryos*, 'cold') + *–phile* (< Gk. *philos*, 'beloved, loving')]

Not everyone nor everything dislikes the cold, of course, and if you're a *cryophile* – or a **psychrophile**, to put it another way

– then you positively love it. Not that you'll find a great many of these among humankind, however, as both these terms originated in the worlds of biology and zoology, and were first applied to specialist organisms capable of living and thriving at extremely cold temperatures.

cuff (*v.*) to beat one's arms against one's sides to keep warm [1785; < *cuff*, 'to hit']

The verb *cuff* has been used more loosely to mean to strike or hit since the 1500s, but it has amassed a variety of other more specific meanings over the years, including to exchange gossipy tittle-tattle, to secrete something inside your hand, and this wintry expression from the late eighteenth century. Oddly, in this context the term often formed part of a fuller phrase, *to cuff Jonas* (with Jonas apparently acting as little more than a generic John Doe-style name for oneself). Odder still, in the sense of two flailing limbs knocking together, *cuff Jonas* could also be used of 'one who is knock-kneed', according to Francis Grose's 1785 *Dictionary of the Vulgar Tongue*, while beating one's arms against one's sides has also been known as 'two thieves beating a rogue' and, among nineteenth-century sailors at least, 'beating the booby'.

See also **barflog, slappaty-pouch**

degombling (*n.*) the act of knocking accumulations of snow from your shoes after walking outdoors in wintertime [Antarctic sl., 2000; < *de–* + *gomble*, 'ball of snow']

See **gomble**

dingle (*n.*) a fine winter's day, in which visibility or travel is pleasant despite the icy conditions; (*adj.*) of winter weather: noticeably fine and clear [Antarctic sl., 1989; of unknown origin, ? < Bob Dingle, polar researcher]

Why *dingle*? Well, given that this term (like **degombling**) was coined by Antarctic research scientists, who seem to have a propensity for somewhat random inventions, goodness only knows. There is a curious clutch of place names dotted around the Antarctic coastline that share this name, however, including Dingle Lake (a saltwater glacial lake discovered in the mid 1930s) and Dingle Dome (a dome-shaped glacier, discovered in 1956), both of which were named either by or in honour of an Australian meteorologist and polar researcher named Bob Dingle (1920–2016). Is the etymological implication here that the weather is so fine – and therefore, visibility so good – that someone standing at the South Pole could see all the way to the coast? It's as good a guess as any.

dirler (*n.*) an especially keen or hard frost that causes the extremities to tingle [1923; < *dirl*, 'to pierce, to cut through; to make felt']

Recorded in local Scots and North Country vocabularies since the sixteenth century, to *dirl* essentially means to tingle or throb dully (either pleasantly or unpleasantly – like the sensation of knocking your funny bone, according to one nineteenth-century definition). A frost or chill in the air that causes just such a tingling sensation can be known as a *dirler*.

dobble (*n.*) a ball of snow that clings to the shoes, clothing or fur of an animal [1895; ? < *daub*]

Perhaps a dialect extension of *daub*, the word *dobble* is an East Anglianism that as well as meaning a ball of snow can apparently also be used of a messy, clinging clod of mud or wet earth. As a verb, alternatively, to *dobble* is to dig or use a garden tool in a feeble or ineffectual way, while if the soil itself is *dobbly*, then it's too wet to be workable.

See also **gomble**

feetings (*n. pl.*) fellow walkers' or animals' tracks left in a field of snow [1853; < *feet*]

If you're out and about in winter early enough to **break the brod** of an untouched snowfield, then perhaps the only *feetings* you'll see will be those of birds and animals.

> *There were no 'feetings' – no tracks of travellers who had gone before me; I was the first man to tread the snow that day. This was no trifling affair. It is nothing in a town street . . . but in the Moors, untrodden snow is not to be laughed at.*
>
> James Kendall, *Rambles of an Evangelist* (1853)

frigolabile (*adj.*) susceptible to or liable to change in cold temperatures [1917; < *frigo–* (< Lat. *frigor*, 'cold') + *labile*, 'prone to change' (< Lat. *labilis*, 'transient')]

frigostable (*adj.*) resistant to or unaffected by the cold [1918; < *frigo–* (< Lat. *frigor*, 'cold') + *stable*]

A pair of opposite terms from the material sciences that are more strictly used in relation to the physical resistance and transmutability of various substances. Whether they're worth utilising in a different context in winter temperatures rather depends on whether the first or the second best describes how **coldrife** you are.

gawmless (*adj.*) clumsy, due to having the fingers benumbed with cold [1775; ? < *gawm*, 'to grasp']

Nothing to do with being *gormless*, the 'gawm' rooted in this word likely comes from an even earlier seventeenth-century word, *gawm* or *gaum*, meaning to hold onto or to grasp. So if you're *gawmless*, you're ultimately unable to get your chilled and benumbed fingers to operate as they should.

gomble (*n.*) an accumulation of snow, as in a person's hair or an animal's fur [Antarctic sl., 2000; of unknown origin]

You can thank the ever-inventive minds of Antarctic research scientists for this word too. They seemingly came up with the entirely random coinage *gomble* sometime in the late 1990s, to describe a frozen accretion of ice or snow that sticks to hair, shoes or clothing in cold weather. By extension, that makes **degombling** the act of knocking or brushing accumulations of snow from yourself when you return indoors in wintry weather.

See also **dobble**

hirple, hurple (*v.*) to walk with hunched shoulders because of the cold [15thC; ? < rel. Dut. *hurken*, 'squat']

Logophiles love the verb *hurple*, because it is one of only a handful that rhyme with the colour *purple* (the others being *curple*, an encircling leather strap on a saddle, and *besperple*, meaning to splash). Thought to be at least related to older Dutch and German roots meaning to crouch or squat, *hurple* has been in recorded use in English since the 1400s in various senses referring to contracting or drawing in the limbs 'with pain or cold', or 'like a beast in a storm', according to the *Oxford English Dictionary*.

See also **hunch-weather**

ice-bolt (*n.*) a sudden chill or piercing sensation of cold; an avalanche [1789; *ice* + *bolt*, 'something moving rapidly']

There is an unexpected and shocking attack of something cold wrapped up in both definitions of the word *ice-bolt*, albeit with one being rather more catastrophic than the other. The former, meaning a sudden chill, is the older of the two, recorded in various poetic contexts in the late 1700s; the latter, meaning an avalanche, emerged in the early 1800s.

ice-legs (*n.*) the ability to keep one's balance while walking on ice [1854; *ice* + *legs*, modelled on earlier *sea-legs*]

If a sailor's *sea-legs* are what keep him upright and acclimatised to life on board a ship, then someone out and about in wintertime needs to develop a good set of *ice-legs* to ensure they can walk safely across frozen, slippery ground.

> *It is difficult to gain sea-legs, but to accomplish ice-legs is yet more difficult.*
>
> W. B. Jerrold, *A Brage-Beaker with the Swedes* (1854)

See also **icemanship**, **pote**

icemanship (*n.*) skill in crossing or dealing with icy ground [1865; < *iceman*, 'someone skilled in travelling in frozen regions' + *–ship*]

If you think this word and its cousin **snowmanship** sound like jokey modern inventions, think again: both were coined in the mid nineteenth century, originally in the context of alpine mountaineering. Although invented independently, they both follow much the same template as other somewhat older words for shows of skill or dexterity, such as *penmanship* and *craftsmanship*.

See also **ice-legs**

impluviousness (*n.*) the state of being rain-soaked [1727; < earlier *impluvious* (1656) < *im*– (< Lat. *in*–, 'in, upon') + *pluvious*, 'relating to rain' (< Lat. *pluvia*, 'rain')]

The wintertime isn't all about snow and ice, of course – sometimes it rains too. For that there is this eighteenth-century coinage for the state or condition of being thoroughly wet through, which in turn comes from an older equivalent adjective, *impluvious*, defined as 'wet with rain' in a dictionary of 1656.

jurpit (*v.*) to walk across frozen or snow-covered ground by stepping into another person's footprints, in an attempt not to slip [dial., 1809; ? < *chur*, 'to leap, to step broadly' + *pit*, 'indentation']

If you haven't quite got your **ice-legs** yet, then perhaps *jurpitting* your way across snowy or icy ground is your best bet. This bizarre and somewhat unlikely sounding dialect term apparently refers to the practice of following or stepping in another person's footprints, in an attempt to remain safely upright (because surely if they made it across the snow without falling, then so can you. . .) As curious a word as this is, it is likely nothing more than a local combination of an earlier dialect verb to *chur*, or *jurr*, meaning to walk or bound with broad steps, plus the noun *pit*, in this sense presumably referring to each foot's indentation in the snow.

> *To JURPIT . . .* [is] *to pace as another does, by safely striding into his footprints across snow covered ground in winter.*
>
> G. P. Howard, *A Glossary . . . of the Northern Counties* (1809)

kittly-benders (*n.*) a game in which people run over thin or bending ice [US dial., 1854; ? < *kittle*, 'to tickle']

To *kittle* is to tickle, so if you're *kittly* then you're ticklish. A patch of enticingly fragile or bendable ground ice consequently became known as *kittly-benders* in American regional English in the mid nineteenth century, and from there a game of the same name emerged soon after, in which players attempt to race across a patch of 'kittly' ice without it breaking.

maggle (*v.*) to trudge laboriously through thick snow [Sc., *c.* 1810; < earlier Sc. *maggle*, 'to hinder']

In more general terms, the Scots word *maggle* essentially means merely to blunder or struggle, or else to cause an inconvenience.

> *To maggle is common Scotish* [sic] *for impede; as he was maggled with or by his wet clothes, his feet were maggled by the deep snow, the mire and deep roads maggled him.*
>
> Alexander Murray, *History of the European Languages* (1823)

See also **post-hole**

meldrop (*n.*) a single drop from the tip of a melting icicle; a drop from the tip of a cold person's nose [OE; < rel. OE *mǽl*, 'phlegm']

It might be tempting to presume this is a contraction of 'melt-drop', but the sheer age of this word proves that to be wrong. In fact, the first part of it is believed to be an ancient Scandinavian borrowing that has been in use in English since the time of the Vikings: the 'mel–' here is actually some kind of early Nordic word for the bit of a horse's bridle, and appropriately enough one of this word's oldest meanings was a droplet of foaming saliva that forms at a horse's mouth.

niphablepsia (*n.*) snow-blindness [? 1800s; < Gk. *nipha*, 'snow' + *ablepsia*, 'blindness']

Niphablepsia is just one form of a painful eye condition known as *photokeratitis*, in which unprotected eyes are exposed to damaging levels of ultraviolet light, causing the eyes' sensitive inner layers to essentially become sunburned. In winter weather, it is less the intensity of the sun itself that causes a problem than its reflection off a dazzling blanket of snow.

peck of apples (*n.*) a heavy, clumsy fall on ice [dial., 1866; <*peck*, 'large mass or quantity']

A *peck* is a barrel, or a relatively large unit of capacity, and it is likely in the sense of a large, weighty, cumbersome object that the phrase *peck of apples* came to be used of a clumsy fall on icy ground in the mid nineteenth century.

peel (*v.*) to travel in bad weather dressed in ill-suited clothing [dial., 1824; < peel-the-bones]

peel-a-flee (*n.*) someone unsuitably dressed for the winter weather [dial., 1825; <*peel*, 'to remove']

peelringe (*n.*) someone who has become utterly stupefied with cold [Sc., 1923 ? < peel]

Peel-the-bones is a suitably evocative term for a piercingly cold wind or period of winter weather, in the sense that it feels cold enough outside to literally 'peel' the flesh from your bones. The three regional words listed here are all rooted in the same idea, and are all likely in some way related to one another.

To *peel* is to travel or venture out in cold weather in inadequate or unsuitable clothing – or to be 'travelling in a windy, wild day, with light clothes on', according to one 1824 definition. A *peel-a-flee* (literally, 'a fly stripped of its wings') is someone attired in just such an unsuitable way; originally, it described a foppish dandy whose choice of clothes made him stand out from the crowd. And a *peelringe* is 'a person appearing stupefied with intense cold', according to a 1923 guide to the dialect of Roxburghshire – or, as the *Scottish National Dictionary* somewhat less sympathetically puts it, 'a thin-blooded shivering skinny person'.

post-hole (*v.*) to walk in snow deep enough for your legs to sink into it with each step [? US, late 20thC; < *post*, 'stake' + *hole*]

In literal terms, a *post-hole* is nothing more than a hole in the ground left by or dug out for a fence post or wooden stake. *Post-holing* – a term from hiking and mountaineering – therefore implies walking or trudging across snowy ground in such a way that you leave a series of deep leg-shaped indentations, rather like a row of post-holes, behind you.

See also **jurpit**, **maggle**

pote (*v.*) to walk slowly or unsteadily on frozen ground [? OE; < *pote*, 'to walk carefully']

An ancient word that appears to be largely confined to dialect today, *pote* has been in use for centuries in various senses referring to walking, kicking, pawing the ground or placing the feet in some specific or careful manner. The sense here of walking slowly across frozen and slippery ground is recorded in a handful of nineteenth-century dialect dictionaries, but given the word's age we can presume it has been in use locally in this way considerably longer than that.

See also **ice-legs**

psychrophile (*n.*) something or someone who enjoys or thrives in very cold temperatures [1906; < *psychro–* (< Gk. *psychros*, 'cold, frozen') + *–phile* (< Gk. *philos*, 'beloved, loving')]

See **cryophile**

scringing (*n.*, *v.*) the crackling sound that ice or frozen ground makes when someone walks across it [1896; ? < onomatopoeic]

Scringe, an etymological cousin of *cringe*, is a superbly evocative verb dating from the seventeenth century used of all manner of sounds and sensations relating to crushing, contracting, flinching, clenching or otherwise knotting or pushing together. This definition may simply be an extension of all the others (perhaps in the sense of the ice or frost 'flinching' or 'contracting' below someone's weight), or it may be no relation at all, perhaps nothing more than onomatopoeia. As well as cracking or crackling like ice, the *English Dialect Dictionary* explains, *scringe* can also be used of a creaking or grating sound – or the uncomfortable nails-down-a-blackboard sensation caused by just such a noise:

> *When a boy sharpens his slate-pencil with a knife, he says it makes his teeth 'scringe'.*
>
> F. M. T. Palgrave, *Words and Phrases . . . of Hetton-le-Hole* (1896)

scrumpety (*adj.*) of the ground: frozen with the first hard frost of winter [1898; < *scrump*, 'to crunch' (< onomatopoeic)]

To *scrump* is to eat greedily or noisily, and it is likely in the sense of audibly crunching and crackling that in the nineteenth century the adjective *scrumpety* came to be used of hard frozen ground.

scudder (*v.*) to slide on ice or snow [dial., 1882; ? < *scud*, 'to move briskly']

As well as meaning to slide – either intentionally or otherwise – on frozen ground, *scudder* can also be used as a noun for a driving wintry shower of rain or sleet.

shell (*v.*) of the fleece of a sheep, to become caked in snow [Sc., dial., *c.* 1800; < *shell*, 'hard outer casing']

Take a walk in the country on a snowy day and you may well see shelled sheep resolutely seeing out the winter on isolated hillsides. 'To have snow lodge among the tops of the wool and freeze like an incrustation' is how the *English Dialect Dictionary* defines this rather specific use of the word *shell*, which has likely been in use locally since at least the 1700s.

sitzmark (*n.*) the impression left in snow by a skier falling backwards [*c.* 1930; < Ger. *sitzen* 'to sit' + *mark*, 'indentation']

The fact that this word is a curiously international combination of the German for sit and the English *mark* suggests that it might have been coined by, or else in reference to, somewhat less experienced English-speaking skiers in German-speaking ski resorts. It dates from sometime in the early twentieth century.

slappaty-pouch (*n.*) the act of hitting your arms against your sides and legs to keep warm in cold weather [1702; < *slap*, 'to strike' + *pouch*, 'pocket']

Proving that there really may well be a word for everything, slapping your hands against your sides in a vain attempt to warm yourself up is called *slappaty-pouch*. In the sense of striking the sides of the body, it is thought this word is essentially a mangling of 'slap the pockets'.

See also **barflog, cuff**

slare (*n.*) a mark made on ice by someone slipping on it [dial., 1887; < *slare*, 'to step']

Slare is a curious word recorded in a huge number of senses covering more than 300 years, almost all of which refer to some action of stepping, slipping or sliding across something. As well as being a mark left by a slide on ice (**strike a candle**), to *slare* can also be used to mean to deliberately slide across a frozen surface – or, according to one 1877 Lincolnshire dialect dictionary at least, 'to make a noise by rubbing the boot-soles on an uncarpeted floor'.

snape (*v.*) to nip or bite with cold [dial., 1631; < ON sneypa, 'shame']

Adopted from Scandinavian roots in the Middle English period, to *snape*, or *snaple*, originally meant to harm, to rebuke or else to check or restrain in some way. It is perhaps in this sense of holding something back that in the seventeenth century it came to be used of the action of a particularly biting frost or blight that might 'check' the growth of a plant – and ultimately, to nip or bite with exposure to the cold.

snaw-breist (*n.*) a snow-topped hill [Sc., 1919; < Sc. *snaw*, 'snow' + Sc. *briest*, 'breast']

Snaw, unsurprisingly, is just a Scots word for snow, while *breist* here is the equivalent of breast, in the sense of the topmost or frontmost part of something (as in a *chimney-breast*). Put together, a *snaw-breist* is a snow-topped hill or ridge of land, of which countless examples can be found across Scotland at the height of wintertime.

snotsicle (*n.*) an icy drip from a person's nose in cold weather [1997; < *snot* + *icicle*]

Another word credited to polar scientists, who first used it to refer not to a drop from a running nose, but to a nasal stream that has become frozen solid in the extreme cold. Mercifully, temperatures tend not to plunge quite so low outside of the polar areas, hence this word's meaning has defrosted as its use has spread into more temperate regions, embraced by everyone from cross-country skiers to wintertime hikers.

snow-blunt (*n.*) a short, heavy fall of snow [dial., 1893; < *blunt*, 'curt, abrupt']

The adjective *blunt* has been used as a noun to mean an appropriately 'blunt' (i.e. heavy and unceremoniously short-lasting) storm of any kind since the early 1800s.

snow-bones (*n.*) the long white lines of untouched snow left on a road between the tracks of vehicles [1814]

This brilliantly imaginative word for the long, pristine lines of white snow that run down winter roads was likely in use locally in the 1700s at least, before first finding its way into print in an 1814 *Provincial Glossary*. As well as lines of snow left between the tracks of vehicles, *snow-bones* can also be used of the snow that fills the ploughed furrows and long surrounding ditches of farmers' fields.

snowmanship (*n.*) a person's ability to walk safely across snowy or wintry ground [1869]

See **icemanship**

stivven (*adj.*) blocked with snow [Sc., ? 19thC; < Sc. *stivven*, 'stiffen']

This is the Scots form of *stiffen*, and as well as describing a road or route that has become 'stivvened' with snow, it can also be used of hands that have become numb and immobile with the winter cold.

strike a candle, to (*v. phr.*) to slide on ice and leave a mark on the ground where you slid [1898; < the long white mark left on the ice]

This expression seems to have been used both of accidental icy slips and of the marks left by children deliberately sliding on frozen ground, with a heel dug into the surface behind them in an attempt to leave as long a mark as possible. In the sense of leaving a long, pale, waxy-looking streak on the ground behind you, meanwhile, another nineteenth-century expression for precisely the same embarrassment/childhood feat was *to strike bacon*.

weather-fast (*adj.*) detained by bad weather [1855; < *weather* + *fast*, 'stuck']

Fast is a prime example of a quirk of language known as a contronym – a word with two or more opposing senses, in this case 'moving rapidly' and 'utterly immobile' (as in 'stuck fast'). It is the latter that is found in this expression, meaning 'confined or detained by stress of weather', according to an 1868 *Glossary of the Cleveland Dialect*. Long before its reappearance in the mid 1800s, however, the equivalent Old English term *wederfæst* was in recorded use way back in the eleventh century.

winterbourne (*n.*) an intermittent stream that only flows during the winter months [OE; < *winter* + *bourne* (< *burn*, 'stream')]

Commonly found on chalklands (where it is often also used as a place name), so-called *winterbourne* streams appear only in months when rain and melted snow cause the level of the groundwater to rise above that of the valley floor, feeding the stream.

winterpiece (*n.*) a picture or image of a wintry landscape [1797; < *winter* + *piece*, 'artwork']

As well as being used of scenic photographs and works of art, the term *winterpiece* can also be applied to an especially evocative poem or written description of the wintertime (a sense that dates back even further, to the early 1600s).

See also **icescape**

6. THE WINTER BLUES

For some of us winter – and the festive period in particular – is not an easy time of year. Perhaps the dark nights are your winter nemesis, and a touch of seasonal affective disorder leaves you feeling flat and down as the year approaches its end. Maybe you keep succumbing to the innumerable seasonal viruses floating around, and so find yourself tucked up early in bed with a warm drink and a hot-water bottle. Or it might be that you've recently gone through a break-up or bereavement, making the run-up to Christmas all the more painful. Whatever it is that has laid you low, you can try to find solace in the words in this chapter dedicated to the feelings, causes and possible solutions to the winter blues.

alysm (*n.*) the restless boredom that comes from being unwell or confined to your bed [1825; < Gk. *alysmos*, 'restlessness, distress']

No one wants to be unwell, but falling ill around Christmas when there is so much to do and so many people to catch up with can be as time-wastingly frustrating as it is downright unpleasant. The uneasy boredom that comes of being confined to your sickbed at any time of year is neatly summed up in *alysm*, or *alysmus*, a word adopted into English from classical medical literature around the turn of the nineteenth century. Derived from a Greek word meaning anguish or distress, *alysm* has an impressive heritage: both it and the very first descriptions of this kind of restlessness are credited to the ancient Greek physician Hippocrates.

brumation (*n.*) wintertime sluggishness, a semi-dormant decrease in activity during the winter months [1965; < Lat. *bruma*, 'winter']

Rather than fully hibernate during the winter, some creatures go into a vague state of torpor known as *brumation*. They are not asleep, as true hibernators are, but simply slow down and maintain only the most basic of bodily functions, seeing out the winter months in this sluggish, inactive, semi-dormant state until they are roused by the warmer sunlight and temperatures of the spring. And if all that sounds familiar at this time of year, then perhaps this term from the fields of ecology and zoology is worth extending into humankind too.

See also **hiemate**, **snowbird**

cheimaphobia (*n.*) a fear or intense dislike of the winter [1931; < Gk. *cheima*, 'coldness, wintertime' + *–phobia* (< Gk. *phobos*, 'fear')]

A dislike of cold conditions can also variously be known as *frigophobia*, *cryophobia* or *psychropophobia* – while if it's the dark nights that get to you, you may well have a touch of **lygophobia** instead.

Christmas compliments (*n.*) a cough, chilblains and a runny nose [1786]

In eighteenth- and nineteenth-century slang, this expression emerged to describe a standard trio of undesirable consequences of the worst of the winter weather: 'A cough, kibed [i.e. chilblained] heels, and a snotty nose', as Francis Grose's *Dictionary of the Vulgar Tongue* explained it in the late 1700s.

clinomania (*n.*) an excessive desire to lie down [1939; < *clino–* (< Gk. *clino*, 'to lean') + *–mania* (< Gk. *mania*, 'madness')]

'A morbid desire to lie in bed, or at least in a horizontal position' is how one dictionary defined this back in the 1940s. First used in European medical literature in the late nineteenth century (in the not-so-light-hearted context of depressive disorders and mental instability), the online zeal for obscure words has seen *clinomania* reinvented in recent decades as a wholly relatable state of mind in the modern world. And with both dark nights and dark mornings to contend with, perhaps there is nothing too morbid at all about wanting to remain in bed in the gloomy depths of winter.

See also **dysania, lypophrenia**

crazzler (*n.*) a trying, testing experience [dial., 1876; ? < rel. *craze*]

'A thing that tests one's capacities, or one's powers of endurance, such as a difficult task or an influenza cold' is how the *English Dialect Dictionary* defines a *crazzler*, a word pinpointed to the mid-Yorkshire region in particular. Quite where it comes from etymologically, however, is a mystery, though in the sense of something that drives a person mad (in all senses of the word), *crazzler* is perhaps somehow related to *craze*.

crymodynia (*n.*) pain caused or worsened by cold temperatures [1851; < *crymo–* (< Gk. *crymos*, 'cold') + *–odynia* (< Gk. *odyne*, 'pain, anguish')]

Crymodynia was originally used in nineteenth-century medical literature as an alternative name for chronic rheumatism, which many sufferers feel is brought on or exacerbated by chilly temperatures.

Fittingly enough, the word combines a pair of Greek roots that literally mean 'cold pain'.

dysania (*n.*) difficulty getting up in the morning [1958; < Gk. *dys–*, 'bad, difficult' + ? Gk. *ania*, 'distress, trouble']

For the non-vampiric among us, the winter can leave us craving even the merest glimpse of sunlight. And while **clinomania** might be a simple desire to lie down or go to bed, *dysania* is the opposite: a seemingly insuperable difficulty in getting out of bed after you have woken up.

ergasthenia (*n.*) exhaustion from overworking [1918; < *ergo–* (< Gk. *ergon*, 'work') + Gk. *astheneia*, 'weakness']

Preparing everything for Christmas can be stressful enough, but add to that all the usual everyday tasks and stresses of work, and it is understandable that many of us may feel a little burned out as the year-end approaches. If that's the case, a word well worth remembering is *ergasthenia* – a turn-of-the-century medical term that literally means 'work-weakness'.

fat sorrow (*n.*) sadness alleviated by material things [1507]

German is one of those languages popularly said to have a word for everything, and *kummerspeck* (literally, 'bacon-fat grief') is a superbly evocative term for excess weight gained by comfort eating. Despite our own language being similarly well furnished, alas it doesn't have a precise equivalent, but *fat sorrow* is certainly in the same ballpark.

Immortalised in an old Tudor-period adage advising that 'Fat sorrow is better than lean sorrow', this word alludes to a feeling of sadness or wretchedness that can be eased by riches or material things. So when you find yourself indulging in a little treat to lift your mood in the wintertime, this is the word you're after.

forwintered (*adj.*) worn out by the winter months [1481; <*for–* + *wintered*]

As well as being used to intensify the frostiness of **forfrorn**, the prefix *for–* also appears in a group of words implying some sense of being utterly broken by something – or, in the words of the *Oxford English Dictionary*, 'reduced to straits'. It is this that appears in the excellent fifteenth-century word *forwintered*, which can be used to describe anything or anyone feeling appropriately drained or depleted by the long winter months.

lygophobia (*n.*) a fear or hatred of darkness or gloominess [1955; < Gk. *lyge*, 'twilight' + *–phobia* (< Gk. *phobos*, 'fear')]

If your heart sinks as the nights begin to draw in, then perhaps you are a *lygophobe*.

See also **cheimaphobia**

lypophrenia (*n.*) causeless sadness or melancholy [? *c.* 1967; < Gk. *leipo*, 'to fail, to be lacking' + *–phrenia*, 'psychological disorder, state of mind' (< Gk. *phren*, 'mind')]

One of the cruellest things about the winter blues is that they tend to kick in either side of what we're told is The Most Wonderful Time of the Year. The Christmas period is one of festivities and fellow-feeling, so it can seem unsettlingly out of place to feel down at the tail end of the year when there is ostensibly so little reason for it. *Lypophrenia*, or *lipophrenia*, is apparently the word for just this kind of disquiet: look it up online, and you'll find it widely defined as 'a feeling of vague sadness, seemingly without cause'.

That being said, there is a rather knotty story behind this word that suggests that definition should be taken not just with a pinch of salt, but with an entire road gritter. *Lypophrenia* appears to have been first defined in those terms in *Mrs Byrne's Dictionary*, a light-hearted collection of unusual words published in 1974. Such was that book's success that practically every collection of linguistic oddities since has followed suit and replicated its definition almost word for word: five decades on and this 'feeling of vague sadness' is now so virally relatable that a quick Google of *lypophrenia* will bring up Mrs Byrne's definition reproduced everywhere from TikTok videos to T-shirts. The turn-of-the-century physicians who actually *used* this word, however, had a very different idea of it.

'Failure of mental capacity' is how one 1905 dictionary defined *lypophrenia*. Another called it 'chronic dementia'. Even the hallowed medical journal *The Lancet* got in on the act in 1899, explaining this as a rather grave catch-all term for 'terminal conditions of mental dissolution secondary to previous insanities'. A 'feeling of vague sadness' this is not.

So what has happened? Did the term weaken somehow between the 1800s and the mid 1970s? Apparently not, given that medical dictionaries and psychiatric journals alike continue to use the word as they always have, referring not to a melancholic state of mind but a dementia-like decline of faculties. Instead, the problem seems to lie with a 1967 *Layman's Dictionary of Psychiatry* that wrongly defined both *lypophrenia* (mental decline) and *lypothymia* (a feeling of faintness) as merely 'melancholia' – and in doing so, seems to have confused them both with an entirely different condition, *lypomania* (which really *is* pathological melancholy). Despite the error, Mrs Byrne and the other writers who followed her seemingly took that definition and ran with it, creating the viral 'feeling of vague sadness' that the internet loves so much today. Alas, the genie cannot be put back in the bottle, and this new meaning, despite its inaccuracy, is now so widespread that it can scarcely be ignored (hence its inclusion here). But perhaps the moral of this tale is that it is never wise to believe everything you read on the internet. Nor, for that matter, on a T-shirt.

maulifuff (*n.*) a woman devoid of energy, or who appears to keep herself busy but achieves nothing [Sc., 1808 < *Molly* + ? *fuff*, 'wisp, puff']

The first part of this word comes from the girl's name *Molly* (used here as a generic name for any woman), while a *fuff* is a slight puff of air, or anything so wispy and unsubstantial that it could easily be moved by one. Put together, they make a curious word for a similarly light and ineffectual person, or else someone so utterly spent and exhausted that they are a mere wisp of their former self.

matutolypea (*n.*) a feeling of grumpiness or downheartedness first thing in the morning [1958; < *Mater Matuta*, Roman goddess of the morning + Gk. *lype*, 'grief']

Mater Matuta was a Roman goddess of the morning, whose name in this odd word has been attached to *lype*, a Greek word for grief or mourning. 'Morning mourning' is hardly the most artful of word formations, but in essence *matutolypea* is a classically educated version of getting out of the wrong side of the bed – a word for the glummest, darkest mornings of the wintertime.

See also **matutinal**

meteorotropism (*n.*) the notion that the weather can affect people's health and wellbeing; an instance of this [1935; < *meteoro–*, 'weather-related' (< Gk. *meteoros*, 'high, elevated') + *–tropism*, 'growth, movement' (< Gk. *tropos*, 'a turning')]

The weather can certainly affect physical conditions, but anyone feeling more than a little glum beneath the rainy and sunless skies of winter will no doubt feel this term can be applied just as much to their state of mind as to their body.

See also **cyclonopathy**

merry-go-sorry (*n.*) a mixture of joy and unhappiness [1599]

A term apparently coined by sixteenth-century writer Nicholas Breton, whose works provide the only written records of it, *merry-go-sorry* is the English equivalent of what might also be known as *chantepleure* (from the French for 'singing' and 'crying') or, in medical parlance at least, *dacrygelosis* (from a pair of Greek roots meaning 'tears' and 'laughter'). Of the three, it is perhaps the less melodramatic English version that best sums up the melancholy of a festive period not spent how or with whom one would wish, and the strange contradictory feeling of enjoying yourself at Christmas when your mind or your loved ones are elsewhere.

misslieness (*n.*) a feeling of loneliness caused by the absence of something or someone who is usually around [Sc., 1825; < *missly*, *misslie*, 'lonely, missing someone']

There can be a lonesome aspect to the winter blues, especially if someone you know or love is not or no longer around at Christmastime. The Scots word *misslieness* neatly sums this feeling up, defined by the Scottish lexicographer John Jamieson as 'solitariness, from the absence of some favourite person or thing'.

Given that sufficient people have experienced this feeling for it to have been given a name, however, it is a nice reminder that you are never alone in your loneliness – while the fact that Jamieson's definition was penned way back in 1825 proves this feeling is by no means new.

mubble-fubbles (*n.*) a period of low spirits [1589; ? < rel. mulligrubs]

Sing-songy expressions comprised of two rhyming or mirroring parts like this are sometimes known as ricochet words, and their back-and-forth construction seems especially suited to terms describing some feeling of uncertainty, indifference and melancholy. To be *frobly-mobly*, for instance, is to be indifferently well – that is, neither well nor unwell, but just generally out of sorts. Likewise, you can feel *deetle-dottle* (befuddled, unsure), *huten-truten* (ill-tempered, sulky), *crawly-mawly* (in ailing health) or *parry-marry* (weak, insipid). The *Scottish National Dictionary* variously defines *hingum-tringum* as 'in low spirits', 'barely presentable' or 'just hanging together'. You might be suffering through a bout of *screwton-newtons* if you have 'a miserable feeling in body and mind', according to an 1896 dictionary of the Warwickshire dialect. Or you may merely be in your *mubble-fubbles*, a sixteenth-century name for general low spirits. Quite where this bizarre word comes from is anyone's guess, but given the implications here, there may be some distant connection to the next word on this list, **mulligrubs**.

mulligrubs (*n.*) a fit of ill-temperedness [1599; ? < *grubs*, 'larvae, parasites']

As well as meaning a period of low spirits or ill temper, since the seventeenth century *mulligrubs* has also been used to refer to a feeling of queasiness, or an upset stomach. That second meaning has led to the etymological suggestion that the 'grubs' lurking here might be the same larvae that can infest food and cause digestive upset – which is certainly more than enough to ruin your usually even temperament.

Novemberish (*adj.*) gloomy, melancholic [1793]

If proof were ever needed of the gloominess of the winter months, the adjective *Novemberish* has been used for more than 200 years to describe anything as dismally 'characteristic of November', according to the *Oxford English Dictionary*.

> *Here I sit, altogether Novemberish, a damn'd melange of Fretfulness & melancholy, not enough of the one to rouse me to passion; nor of the other to repose me in torpor; my soul flouncing & fluttering round her tenement, like a wild Finch caught amid the horrors of winter newly thrust into a cage.*
>
> Robert Burns, Letter (1793)

See also **Winter Friday**

ombrosalgia (*n.*) a pain that is caused by or that appears to worsen in wet weather [1958; < *ombro–* (< Gk. *ombros*, 'rain shower'] + *–algia* (< Gk. *algos*, 'pain']

See **crymodynia**

physitribia (*n.*) the exhaustion of physical energy [1958; < *physio–* + Gk. *tribe*, 'wearing down, wasting away']

When things get a little too much and you're left utterly devoid of energy, that's *physitribia*. A medical term recorded since the mid

1900s, it rather fittingly derives from a Greek root, *tribe*, that could be used not only of a gradual running down or wearing away, but of something so utterly occupying that it demands all your care and attention. And in the run-up to Christmas in particular, concerns like that are seemingly everywhere.

psychroalgia (*n.*) a painful sensation of the cold [1904; < *psychro–* (< Gk. *psychros*, 'cold, frozen') + *–algia* (< Gk. *algos*, 'pain')]

Not to be confused with *psychalgia* (which is literally a 'pained' mind), *psychroalgia* is an especially painful sensitivity to the cold. In essence, it's a rather more medically tinged version of words like *nesh* and **coldrife**.

snowbird (*n.*) someone who heads to warmer climes to escape the winter [US, 1924]

Originally, a *snowbird* was precisely that: any small migratory bird that was only seen, or only noticed, in wintertime. In Europe, the term emerged in the 1600s and was much used of the snow bunting, while in North America it typically referred to the dark-eyed junco, a sparrow-like bird from the subarctic that winters in the warmer southern and central USA.

In the early 1900s, however, *snowbird* came to be applied to people who likewise relocated in the colder months. At first it referred to dropout soldiers who would enlist in the army in the autumn, use their military status to receive warm clothes, shelter and food during the winter, and then desert in the spring. By the 1920s, the meaning had shifted again to denote construction workers who drifted south during the winter when employment opportunities quite literally froze up in the north. And lastly, and most recently of all, *snowbird* has come to refer to tourists, retirees and other seasonal visitors to the sunnier southern states who arrive in vast numbers in the winter to escape the snow and ice of the north. One solution to the winter blues, it seems, is not to endure them at all.

See also **brumation**, **hiemate**

sullen-sick (*adj.*) feeling physically ill from a downhearted mood or period of melancholy [1614]

If you're the kind of person whose mental upset can manifest itself in a physical way, then you're *sullen-sick* – or 'sick with sulleness', according to the 1895 *Century Dictionary*.

Winter Friday (*n.*) a cold, wretched-looking person [1880]

Another metaphorical reminder of the bleakness of winter, the definition above comes from a 1913 guide to *Rustic Speech and Folklore*, but the expression itself has been in recorded use since the late 1800s.

See also **Novemberish**

wintercearig **(*n.*) a feeling of downheartedness or despondency caused by, or as desolate as, the depths of winter [OE, *c.* 10thC; < OE *winter* + *cearig*, 'causing sorrow']**

Wintercearig is a fiercely evocative word recorded just once in the history of our language: in *The Book of Exeter*, a tenth-century collection of Old English texts, verses, stories and riddles. The book contains a poem entitled 'The Wanderer' (or *Eardstapa*, 'earth-stepper', in its original Old English), in which a lonely exile relates his thoughts as he looks back over the events of his life. And in one of his reminiscences, he recalls how:

ond ic hēan þonan wōd wintercearig ofer waþema gebind

[*And I, abject, from there travelled with winter-sorrow over the ice-bound waves*]

Cearig is the Old English ancestor of our word *chary*, but is itself a derivative of *cearu*, which is the ancestor of *care*. In turn, *care* originally meant grief or sorrow in Old English, but from there its meaning expanded to include anything that proves a mental burden, consumes your thoughts or demands attention. *Chary*, meanwhile, took a different route, and has ended up meaning wary or hesitant. In both instances, the original implications of anxiousness or sorrow have now largely disappeared, but ring through in this most ancient of coinages.

Winter, meanwhile, has always just meant winter, but it is unclear what its implication is meant to be in *wintercearig*. As well as meaning the coldest season of the year, of course, literary English likes to count the passing of time in winters, so as well as meaning 'sorrowed by the winter months', this word could equally be interpreted as 'sorrowed by the passing of too many winters'. Then again, it could simply be intended to imply that the titular Wanderer is feeling as bleak and as miserable as the winter itself – or perhaps a combination of all three.

yeel's-gird (*n.*) festive weeping [Sc., 1881; < Sc. *yeel*, 'yule' + *gird*, 'metal hoop']

Yeel is a Scots variant of 'Yule', while a *gird* in this context is a circular metal loop or hoop, such as might secure the timbers of a barrel. According to a peculiar quirk of Scottish folklore, if a child were to cry on Christmas Day, they would be said to 'brek Yeel's gird' (i.e. 'break the Yule gird'), and as a result there would be much more weeping and lamentation to come in the year ahead.

7. THE PARTY SEASON

'Tis the season to be merry, and there is perhaps nothing more guaranteed to get everyone merry (in both the gleeful and the skinful senses) than a party, along with some festive food and drink. Whether you're hosting your own bash, attending someone else's or heading out for a night on the town, the words in this chapter should have you covered for a fun seasonal gathering with friends, family and workmates.

abligurition (*n.*) excessive spending on food and drink [1724; partly < Lat. *ligurire*, 'to feast']

'Spending in **belly-cheere**' is how one eighteenth-century dictionary defined this word. Hidden in the midst of it is the Latin verb *ligurire*, which variously meant to feast or gorge oneself, to lick up or lick clean, or to be daintily fond of luxuries and delicacies. Because such delicate treats are typically rather expensive, an extended form of that Latin root later came to be used of indulgent, wasteful spending on food and drink, and eventually fell into use as *abligurition* in the dictionaries of the 1700s.

Adam and Eve (*n.*) a party from which guests are ejected at a set time [1858]

What a difference a century or so makes. In the 1600s, an *Adam and Eve* was an orgiastic party at which all the guests danced as shamelessly naked as the biblical first couple. By the 1800s, however, it had become a thoroughly chaste gathering at which all the invitees would be unceremoniously asked to leave at a prearranged time (a reference to the biblical ejection from the Garden of Eden). Perhaps best to make sure your guests know which one of these you have in mind on the invites, or else avoid the confusion altogether by using a different name: as these rather more antisocial nineteenth-century *Adam and Eve* parties typically ended at midnight, they were also known as *Cinderellas*.

apolausticism (*n.*) total devotion to pleasure and enjoyment [1883; < Gk. *apolafstikós*, 'enjoyment, pleasurableness']

The perfect word to describe festive freedom from the ordinary worries and concerns of the rest of the year, *apolausticism* is rooted in a Greek word meaning enjoyment. If you're the kind of person who signs up to this idea, meanwhile, then you're an *apolaustic* – a term that fell into use slightly earlier in the nineteenth century to describe an aesthetic philosophy that prioritises pleasure, beauty and art over all other concerns.

baltiorum (*n.*) a party or social gathering held around a bonfire [1855; ? < Ir. *Baal-tigh-abhrán* ('song of Baal's house')]

Baltiorum is apparently the anglicised title of a traditional Irish melody, *Baal-tigh-abhrán*, that literally means 'song of Baal's house'. A reference to the pagan deity Baal isn't the most festive of etymologies, admittedly, but whether it was via some ancient pre-Christian outdoor ritual or else just a jolly folk tune, by the mid 1800s the word *baltiorum* had come to be used of 'the boisterous merry-making which often accompanies a bonfire', according to one nineteenth-century definition.

barleyhood (*n.*) drunkenness, surliness caused by overdrinking [1529; < *barley*, an ingredient in beer +–*hood*, 'state, condition']

As well as being a Tudor-period word for a fit of drunkenness (or else the grumpy hangover that follows it), *barleyhood* can also be used of a mean drunk's fit of ill-temperedness or cantankerousness.

barrel-sick (*adj.*) made unwell from drinking [18thC]

The use of barrels to store liquor is the origin of this word as well as a handful of others, including *barrelled* (drunk), *barrel-fever* (drunken sickness) and *barrel-wash* (strong or illicit alcohol). *Barrel-sick* is first recorded in a bawdy eighteenth-century Scottish ballad, 'There was a Wee Bit Wiffikie', which tells the story of a little old lady (the 'wiffikie') who, as she walked to the fair, took a gulp of whisky that 'gaed about the wiffie's heart' so she 'began to spew'.

bauson (*n.*) a corpulent person, someone who has recently gained weight [1607; < ME *bauson*, 'badger']

Admittedly, the definition given above is not this word's original or literal meaning, because a *bauson* is actually a badger. In that sense, it comes from an Old French word, *bauzen*, which was borrowed into medieval English to describe any piebald creature, or any animal with black-and-white markings or a white stripe down its face.

It was the badgers' habit of gorging themselves in the late summer and autumn, fattening themselves up ahead of the leaner winter, that saw this word come to be used of a rotund person – or rather, someone who has only recently become more rotund – in the seventeenth century.

benjo (*n.*) a riotous day-long drinking spree [naut. sl., 1909; of unknown origin, ? < It. *buongiorno*]

A term from Victorian naval slang, defined in one 1909 dictionary as 'a riotous holiday' or 'a noisy day in the streets'. The word's origins are unclear, but it may be that the sailors in question liked to start things early: at least one theory claims this may be a slangy corruption of the Italian greeting *buongiorno*, 'good morning'.

bibacity (*n.*) excessive drinking [1623; < Lat. *bibere*, 'to drink']

The 'bib' hiding inside words like *imbibe* and *bibulous* comes from *bibere*, the Latin for to drink (which is also, through the meanderings of etymology, the origin of *beverage*). With the added implication of drinking to excess or overindulgence, it is likewise the origin of this seventeenth-century coinage, which the lexicographer Henry Cockeram first defined as 'outrageous drinking' way back in 1623.

birl (*v.*) to spend money freely or extravagantly on drink; to pour out or ply with drink [OE; < OE *byrle*, 'cupbearer, server']

Birling is an oddly diverse verb that over the centuries has been applied to everything from plying someone with drink to spinning a coin on a tabletop or balancing atop a floating log. Etymologically, however, there are two different *birls* here.

All those that refer to some manner of rapid movement or rotation are a more recent invention, dating from the 1700s, and are probably meant to be onomatopoeic. The use of *birling* in relation to drink is a more ancient coinage, the root of which is thought to lie in an Old English word, *byrle*, for a cupbearer.

block a quiet pub, to (*v. phr.*) of an individual or a group of people: to descend on a small, quiet bar or tavern and remain there all day [1909]

Another festive Victorianism, in this case referring to someone or some people who would remain installed 'in an out-of-the-way public house' for as long as possible, according to a 1909 dictionary of *Passing English of the Victorian Era*.

blue o'clock (*n.*) the early hours of the morning, when a late-night reveller is only just walking home [1909; < *blue*, colour of the lightening sky]

Alluding to a person walking the quiet streets as the sky begins to lighten in the morning, this is a term that was once 'suggestive of rollicking late hours', according to one early twentieth-century explanation.

bonally (*n.*) a drink or toast taken with a friend who is about to depart [*c.* 1478; equivalent to Fr. *bon*, 'good', + *aller*, 'to go']

Literally a 'good going' in French, *bonally* or *bonaillie* appeared in English in the fifteenth century. It remained in infrequent use right through to the 1800s, when it was revived and popularised in the writings of Sir Walter Scott.

bottle-crony (*n.*) a fellow drinker; someone who can always be relied on for a drunken good time [1827; < *bottle* + *crony*, 'intimate friend']

Words for fellow drinkers are by no means rare, but in the party season this term has the added implication of a boon companion

– a good friend with whom you can always expect to have a riotously good time.

See also **compotator**

bummack (*n.*) a large amount of ale, purchased or brewed especially for a party or festive gathering [Sc., 1808; of unknown origin]

According to one early definition, a *bummack*, or *bummock*, may have amounted to as much as 'two bolls' of liquor, which was 'appropriated for the purpose of being drunk at once at a merry meeting'. A *boll* was an old measure of capacity equal in some places to as much as 48 gallons – so two of those would have made a very 'merry meeting' indeed.

buttybrew (*n.*) a social gathering where everyone pays their fair share of the food and drink [dial., 1886; < *butty*, 'colleague' + *brew*, ? 'brewed drink', i.e. ale, beer]

A *butty* was once a colleague or co-worker, or by extension anything shared or co-owned (a *butty-piece*, in nineteenth-century English, for instance, was a field or area of farmland owned by two people). Quite what a *brew* is in this context is less clear, but if it is not a reference to a mixed or figuratively 'brewed up' crowd of people, it may simply allude to a 'brew' of drink.

cherry-merry (*adj.*) merry from drinking; partly or halfway drunk [1769; ? < *cheery*]

Perhaps originally based on 'cheery', and later muddled or deliberately conflated with the cherry-red colour of wine or port, *cherry-merry* emerged in the mid 1700s as a slangy term for the jolly feeling of being only slightly inebriated. A century or so later, it also fell into use as a noun meaning a small amount of money, either given as a gift or included as a bonus or tip on top of a purchase price – just the right amount of cash it might take to get yourself only partly merry.

cold coffee (*n.*) a draft of liquor taken at work [sl., 19thC]

As well as being a slang name for any drink of beer, in the late nineteenth century *cold coffee* came to be used for a draft of liquor taken secretly at work.

> *In some offices, especially in some printing houses, beer is only allowed at certain hours, while coffee is admissible at all times. Coffee-house mugs are therefore kept, and the errand boys go for 'cold coffee'. The coffee-house keeper has the beer ready, and to such an extent was the effort at deception carried that in some cases milk was mixed with the beer to complete the deception.*
>
> J. Redding Ware, *Passing English of the Victorian Era* (1909)

It's worth noting too that *cold coffee* was also Victorian slang for misfortune, which might be close to the truth if you're found drinking on the job.

compotator (*n.*) someone with whom you share or take a drink, a fellow drinker [1731; < Lat. *com–*, 'together' + Lat. *potare*, 'to drink']

Feel free to also call a fellow reveller or drinking companion a *bowl-fellow* (1509), a *cupmate* (1590), a *pot-ally* (1625) and a **bottle-crony** (1824).

crambazzled (*adj.*) prematurely aged from drinking [dial., ? 19thC; of unknown origin]

'An old man exhausted more by vicious indulgences or habits than by age merely' is how a *crambazzle* was defined back in 1868, with the related adjective *crambazzled* first recorded around a century later. Overdo it at the Christmas party or over the festive period and this might well be a word you find yourself taking with you into the new year.

crapulent (*adj.*) feeling the after-effects of overindulgence; sickened or hungover from an excess of food and drink [1656; ultimately < Gk. *craipale*, 'period of drinking; drunkenness, hangover']

Derived via Latin from a Greek word for a drinking bout, this word isn't onomatopoeic, but there's no doubting it sounds like it.

Daft Days (*n.*) the days between Christmas and New Year [1772]

In modern parlance at least, the odd week-long blur between Christmas Day and New Year's Day has become known as the *merryneum*. If you would prefer a less anatomically evocative term, then happily this expression from the eighteenth century fits the bill too. As well as referring to the annual festive period as a whole, the term *Daft Days* can also be used more loosely for any prolonged period of celebration or merriment, or metaphorically for a person's youth.

drink out of *or* see the island, to (*v. phr.*) to drink until the indentation in the bottom of a bottle of wine becomes visible through the sides of the glass [1811]

The dint in the underside of a bottle is properly called the *punt*, but in eighteenth- and nineteenth-century slang, it was an island:

> *The island is the rising bottom of a wine bottle, which appears like an island in the centre, before the bottle is quite empty.*
>
> Francis Grose, *Lexicon Balatronicum* (1811)

drunk's-nest (*n.*) a drinking bout [1875; ? < modelled on *gape's-nest*]

A *gape's-nest* is a gazing-stock, or something or someone that brings everyone together to gawp open-mouthed. In a similar vein, according to the *English Dialect Dictionary*, a *drunk's-nest* is 'an occasion of drunkenness' in which people come together to have a riotously drunken good time.

Dutch feast (*n.*) a party at which the host gets drunk before their guests [1684; < Dut., app. used here as a pejorative]

The long-standing historical rivalry between England and the Netherlands led to *Dutch* being used in all manner of derisive terms in the seventeenth, eighteenth and nineteenth centuries, often in the sense of something that does not go to plan, is carried out in a questionable or slapdash manner or – as is the case in *Dutch courage*, as well as a *Dutch feast* – is fuelled by drink. *Dutch consolation*, for instance, is an expression in which someone who has experienced something dreadful is made to be thankful that the situation is no worse than it already is. A *Dutch reckoning* was 'a bad day's work, all in the wrong', in Victorian naval slang. And a *Dutch auction* is a public sale where an unrealistically high sale price must be lowered to attract the first bidder.

grog-blossom (*n.*) a patch of redness on the skin, and especially on the nose, caused by excess drinking [1791; < *grog*, 'drink, liquor' + *blossom*, 'flush of redness']

'An eruption of inflamed pimples on the nose or face of a man who drinks ardent spirits to excess' is how at least one dictionary somewhat unsubtly defined a *grog-blossom* back in 1889.

hurricane (*n.*) a wild party at a grand house [1746; < earlier *hurricane*, 'vast storm']

The size and wildness of a tropical storm apparently inspired this word for an equally wild party in eighteenth- and nineteenth-century English. A party in which 'the whole house is full from top to bottom' is how a *hurricane* was described in 1779.

mardle (*n.*) a festive drinking party [1858; ? < Fr. *merdaille*, 'dung, a heap of manure']

As a verb, to *mardle* or *maudle* has long been used to mean to gossip or idle away one's time, but in the mid 1800s the word picked up a handful of other senses alluding to time that could arguably be spent on more constructive matters. So as well as meaning to quarrel or to mollycoddle, it also came to signify to 'indulge in merrymaking', according to the *English Dialect Dictionary*, and from there became a word for 'a festive . . . drinking bout'. Its origins are unclear, but there may be a rather unwelcome connection to an earlier Middle English word for a rowdy rabble of people, *mardle*, or *merdale*, the roots of which lie in a decidedly unfestive French word for excrement.

marl (*v.*) to cheer loudly after toasting someone's health [1886; < *marl*, 'chalky earth']

As etymological twists go, this is a peculiar one. *Marl* is a chalky, mineral-rich material that, as well as forming a large part of the White Cliffs of Dover, has long been used as a means of improving the quality of acid soil. As a verb, to *marl* consequently means to dig for or spread this chalky material on the land – work that was once carried out by gangs of agricultural labourers known as *marlers*. And according to an 1877 *Glossary of Cheshire*, it was apparently once local tradition among gangs of *marlers*, 'after receiving any small sum as a present from a chance visitor', to 'stand in a ring and cheer'.

merry-night (*n.*) a party held in a public house at Christmastime [1783]

A term once common across Scotland and northern England, *merry-night* parties typically involved lots of food, drink, cakes and sweet treats, live music and dancing – as well as 'romping, dancing, and kissing', according to the writer Washington Irving.

Mondayish (*n.*) disinclined to work, after a festive or drunken weekend [1804; < *Monday* + *–ish*, 'of the nature of, akin to']

That first day back at work after a heavy weekend is never easy, but with food and drink aplenty over the holidays, the

Monday-morning indisposition can be all the more severe. For just that feeling, there is this early nineteenth-century invention – which oddly started life among clergymen feeling especially tired after a busy Sunday. From there, however, the word appears to have been somewhat hijacked by Victorian-era partygoers to describe the hungover **crapulence** of the end of the weekend.

Newcastle hospitality (*n.*) excessive, almost overbearing, kindness in the form of food and drink [1855]

Trust the Geordies to know how to show everyone a good time. This term for killing someone with kindness – like a host who can never offer enough to their guests – dates back to the mid nineteenth century. It 'no doubt alludes to the ancient drinking customs of Newcastle and Northumberland', according to one contemporary definition, which adds that these are 'customs now, happily, to a great extent laid aside'. Clearly the words of someone who has never been to the Bigg Market.

old-day (*n.*) a day after a party or a celebration, on which nothing constructive is done or achieved [1866]

Ironically, if you're of an age advanced enough that the day after a party needs to be largely written off, that wasted day is an *old-day*:

> *Christmas . . . tailed off with New Year's Day, which of course had its 'auld day', that is, the day after, which was a lazy day devoted to recuperating from the exertions, and from the eating and drinking of the great day itself.*
>
> *Transactions of the Buchan Field Club* (1900)

partykin (*n.*) a little party [1855; < *party* + *–kin*]

In English '–kin' is a diminutive-forming word ending, which makes a *manikin* a little man, a *napkin* a little 'nap' (or cloth) and a *partykin* a little party. You might still need to take an **old-day** off afterwards to recover, of course.

philoxeny (*n.*) hospitality, kindness to strangers [1623; < *philo–* (< Gk. *philos*, 'love') + Gk. *xenos*, 'strange']

If you're the kind of party host who can find room and food for anyone and everyone, then you're the epitome of *philoxeny* – boundless hospitality and a love of entertaining strangers.

See also **xenodochy**

play camels, to (*v. phr.*) to drink too much, or to excess [1909; ? < the liquid-storing capacity of a camel's hump]

Although not recorded in print until the early 1900s, this curious expression is thought to have emerged in Victorian India. A camel's hump contains fat, not water, but the misapprehension that it is actually a vast store of consumed liquid is likely what lies behind this bizarre turn of phrase – either that, or it is a playful reference to a camel's unquenchable thirst when given the opportunity to drink.

pot-parliament (*n.*) a group of drinkers [1529; < *pot*, ? 'drinking vessel' + *parliament*, 'united gathering of people']

A word recorded just once by the *Oxford English Dictionary*, in the somewhat unlikely context of the writings of Henry VIII's chancellor, Sir Thomas More.

pot-wit (*n.*) someone who's only funny when they're drunk [1611; < *pot*, 'drinking vessel']

If you're the kind of drinker who finds a newfound confidence and quick-wittedness after a glass or two, then you're a *pot-wit*. In fact, English has amassed a host of words for the various different stages of drinking and the characteristics of drinkers, from *lion-drunk* (quarrelsomely drunk, 1592) to *rouzy-bouzy* (boisterously drunk, 1693).

pourboire (*n.*) money or a tip intended to be spent on drink [1788; < Fr. lit. 'for drinking']

This French borrowing is the far more sophisticated-sounding equivalent of what had previously been (and presumably still is) known as *drink-money* in English since the 1600s.

primusophobia (*n.*) the fear of being the first person to arrive [1955; < Lat. *primus*, 'first' + *–phobia* (< Gk. *phobos*, 'fear')]

Nobody wants to be the last person standing at a party, but turning up first before the event is in full swing can be just as awkward. Encapsulating the worrisome feeling of being the first guest to arrive is this jokey word, *primusophobia*, which was coined from a mishmash of Latin and Greek roots in the mid 1950s.

quaff-tide (*n.*) the time or season of partying and drinking [1582; < *quaff*, 'to gulp, to drink' + *tide*, 'time of year']

Dry January be damned! Depending on how much of a party season your festive period turns out to be, your *quaff-tide* may well start before Christmas and last well into the new year.

routing day (*n.*) a day suitable for having a party [1751; < *rout*, 'grand party']

A *rout* was a high-society party or get-together back in the days of George II, which in eighteenth-century English made a *routing day* a day on which such a party was or could be held.

rumball (*n.*) a Christmas Eve feast [dial., 1719; ? < St Rumbold]

If you think this word must surely have once referred to a ball-like celebration at which rum was served, think again. A tradition that seems to have started among Kentish fishermen sometime in the unrecorded past, this name is apparently a corruption of that of the infant saint Rumbold of Buckingham, who lived for just three days in 662. Despite his short life, Rumbold exhibited such piety in his seventy-two hours that he warranted the construction of a small chapel on the south coast of England, where a series of offerings in his name on Christmas Eve led to the rumball tradition:

> *An odd custom used by the fishermen of Folkestone . . . They choose eight of the largest and best whitings out of every boat when they come home from that fishery, and sell them apart from the rest; and out of this separate money is a feast made every Christmas Eve, which they call rumball. The master of each boat provides this feast for his own company, so that there are as many different entertainments as there are boats . . . This word is a corruption from 'rumwold'; and they were anciently designed as an offering for St Rumwold.*
>
> John Harris, *The History of Kent* (1719)

St Rumbold reportedly remains the patron saint of Kent's fishermen to this day.

saddler of Bawtry, the (*n.*) someone who (unwisely) turns down the offer of a drink [18thC; < *Bawtry*, nr. Doncaster]

A curious tale in Yorkshire folklore claims that a saddler from the town of Bawtry was condemned to die at the gallows in York. At the time, there was a tradition in place that anyone so sentenced was permitted one final drink at a tavern on the outskirts of the city, but the saddler turned down the offer and so was taken straight from his cell to the gallows and unceremoniously hanged. Had he accepted, the horseman who was on his way with a last-minute reprieve from the justice of the peace would have arrived in time to stop the proceedings and save the saddler's life. As a result, a proverbial warning – 'Don't be like the saddler of Bawtry!' – emerged in local parlance as a means of discouraging someone from turning down a drink.

semibousy (*adj.*) half drunk [1400s; < *semi–* + *bousy* (< *bouse*, 'to drink']

To *bouse*, in medieval English, was to drink copiously, so if you're *bousy*, then you're drunk – and if you're *semibousy*, then you're only half drunk. The original Middle English word (and its contemporary pronunciation) still survives in the word *booze* today.

surveyor of the highways (*n.*) a drunk person walking home [sl., 1786; < their meandering walk]

A 'reeling drunk' is how one eighteenth-century dictionary defined this phrase, with the implication presumably being of someone so well served by festive cheer that they dawdle their way home, with their lolled head facing downwards, and follow such a zigzagging route that they might as well be inspecting the state of the roads as they go.

symposiarch (*n.*) the host or organiser of a drinking party [1603; < Gk. *sympnein*, 'to drink together' + *–arch* (< Gk. *archos*, 'ruler')]

symposiast (*n.*) a fellow reveller or merrymaker [1656; < Gk. *symposiastes*, 'drinking partner' (< Gk. *sympnein*, 'to drink together')]

Although anyone who has to attend them today might disagree, a *symposium* was originally a drinking party. Etymologically, its roots lie in a Greek word meaning 'to drink together', as do these two words for the hosts and attendees of drunken revelries.

trimmings (*n. pl.*) women's secret lunchtime drinking parties [sl., 1897; < *trimmings*, 'tailors' and dressmakers' cuttings']

Changes to liquor laws in the late nineteenth century made it possible for businesses outside of public houses to apply for licences to sell alcohol from their premises. Among those who seemingly decided to augment their business in this way were cloth and linen sellers, whose haberdasheries soon became venues of impromptu wine-fuelled luncheons among women of a certain social standing. To keep the women's merry exploits secret from their husbands, meanwhile, the business owners listed the drinks as 'trimmings' on their bills, and the name quickly stuck as a slangy codename for a boozy lunch.

upsy freeze (*adv.*) of a bout of drinking: to an excessive degree [1592; ? < Dut., lit. 'in the Friesian manner']

This odd expression is apparently an English mangling of the Dutch phrase *op zijn Fries*, meaning 'in the Friesian manner', which drifted across the Channel during the Elizabethan era. Quite what the natives of Friesland (one of the Netherlands' northernmost provinces) did to deserve this reputation is unclear; in the late 1500s, however, to drink *upsy freeze cross* was also to drink a toast with someone with your arms linked together, so perhaps the original implication was more convivial than unduly excessive. The use of both *upsy Dutch* and *upsy English* as bywords for especially strong ale or liquor perhaps muddied the waters (and muddled the drinkers' minds) too.

yule-crush (*n.*) a festive banquet [1873; < *yule* + *crush*, 'festive party']

In the sense of a dense crowding-together of people, the word *crush* has been used of a party or social get-together since at least the early 1800s, with the more specific *yule-crush* first recorded at the end of the nineteenth century.

yule-rant (*n.*) Christmas merrymaking [? 17thC; < *yule* + *rant*, 'raucous festive gathering']

Although these days we're better used to it meaning to bluster bombastically, to *rant* can also mean to make merry or carouse noisily and boisterously, and it's from there that the word came to be used of an equally raucous party in the 1600s. A festive *yule-rant* is not recorded until far later than that in a handful of (chiefly Scots) early twentieth-century dictionaries, but given that the word at its root is so old – and given that raucous festive celebrations are by no means new – we can presume it was in use far earlier than the evidence suggests.

8. PREPARING FOR THE HOLIDAYS

No matter how organised you may be, the days and weeks leading up to the Christmas period are invariably busy. On top of all the usual stresses and responsibilities of work – and getting sufficiently ahead with everything to make sure things run smoothly over the festive shutdown – there is a house to clean, decorations to put up, meals to shop for and prepare, gifts to wrap, cards to send, relatives to pick up and all manner of other things to make ready. From last-minute housework to decorating the home, the words in this section cover the events and errands of an ever-demanding **Bull Week**, as we head into the holiday season.

Boo Helly (*n.*) the fifth day before Christmas [Sc., 1866; < Sc. *boo*, 'cow' + *helly*, 'holiday, festival']

A *boo* is a cow (or else the entire stock of cattle kept on a farm), while a *helly* is a holiday or celebration (and in the sense of time off work was the name once given to the period between Saturday evening and Monday morning). Put together, *Boo Helly* is the name of an ancient festival held on the fifth day before Christmas Day in Shetland and Orkney, the observance of which is supposed to guarantee the health and safety of the herd in the year to come.

See also **Yules, The**

boun (*v.*) **to decorate something with festive evergreen branches [1865; ? < *bound*, 'to make ready']**

Back in the Middle English period, as a verb to *boun* meant to make ready, while as an adjective it meant prepared or organised (making *ready and boun* essentially a medieval equivalent of 'ready and able' or 'ready and willing'). Confusion with the past tense of the verb, *bouned*, apparently led to the adjective gaining a final D as time went by, and so it is *bound* that has come to mean ready to go or fully prepared in English today (which is why we say we're 'homeward bound' when we're fully prepped for our journey home).

As for the verb, over the years it picked up a handful of additional and more specific senses, so that by the sixteenth century it had come to be used to mean not just to prepare oneself, but to dress. And it is presumably from there, in the sense of decorating or 'dressing' the home, that, sometime around the mid 1800s, *boun* came to mean to adorn with evergreen branches.

Bull Week (*n.*) **the week before Christmas [1831]**

While Scotland has its **Yules** ahead of Christmastime, south of the border there are **Calf Week**, **Cow Week** and **Bull Week**. A trio of terms that first gained currency in the factories of South Yorkshire, Calf Week is the third week before Christmas, Cow Week the second and Bull Week the last. The implication is that as the holiday period approached, workers were expected to gradually redouble their efforts on the factory floor, working slightly extended hours in Calf Week, considerably longer hours in Cow Week and practically every waking hour during Bull Week, so that production was not too greatly affected by the Christmas shutdown.

Quite why the weeks were given these names is unclear. Although one theory claims that the factory owners traditionally rewarded their staff for their extra efforts with a whole roast calf, cow and bull at the end of each gruelling week, the names may just as likely be metaphorical, and allude to the size or quantity of the effort required to get through each progressively longer and busier period.

> *Before the passing of the Factory Acts, it was customary in manufacturing districts . . . to indulge in the practice of working very long hours for a period of three weeks before the Christmas holidays. In the first, which was called CALF WEEK, the ordinary hours of work were but slightly exceeded; in the second, or COW WEEK, they were considerably augmented; and in the third, or BULL WEEK, it was common for operatives to spend the greater portion of the twenty-four of each day in their workshops. The practice resulted in extreme exhaustion and – naturally – indulgence to excess in stimulants.*
>
> John Stephen Farmer, *Slang and Its Analogues Past and Present* (*Vol. II*, 1891)

Calf Week (*n.*) the third week before Christmas [1871]

See **Bull Week**

caudle (*v.*) to perform housework in a messy or disorganised manner [1880; ? < Fr. *caudle*, 'gruel-like drink of warmed, sweetened ale']

Adopted into English from French some seven centuries ago at least, a *caudle* is a hot thick drink of warmed wine or ale, typically flavoured with sugar or spices, and thickened with gruel or barley to make a hearty broth. Because this was so often served to young children and invalids as a kind of restorative, *caudle* (and later *coddle*, and finally *mollycoddle*) came to be used as a verb meaning to pamper or overindulge. But it is in the sense of a mingling of random ingredients that in eighteenth-century English it also came to be used to mean to mix together – and then by extension to create a mess, and finally 'to do household work in an untidy manner', according to one definition recorded in 1880. As such, it is the perfect word for the moment you run out of time, energy or both midway through your pre-Christmas domestic clean-up.

charette (*n.*) a period of intense work undertaken to meet a deadline [? early 1900s; < Fr. *charette*, 'wagon, cart']

Still have a lot on your to-do list with the big day fast approaching? Perhaps it's time for a *charette*. Literally meaning a wagon or chariot, in nineteenth-century France *charette* came to be used of a feverish period of work, thanks to a curious tradition once employed at French art schools. With the end-of-term deadline upon them, design and architecture students – especially those at the famed École des Beaux-Arts in Paris – would reportedly pull rowdy all-nighters to ensure their work was submitted on time. As the students beavered away at their desks and in their studios, a dreaded *charette* would be drawn among them and their completed work loaded onto it for submission and review. When the deadline finally arrived, any work that was not placed on the cart was not accepted for submission – while any that was would be assessed, no matter what stage of completion it was at. This feverish rush to make the school's submission date became known as *nuit de charette*, or 'charette night' among the students concerned, and from there the word soon fell into use in English to refer to any similarly intense time-pressed period of work or activity.

Cow Week (*n.*) the second week before Christmas [1871]

See **Bull Week**

demob-happy (*adj.*) elated that you are about to be released from some arduous or unpleasant employment [1958; < *demob*, 'military demobilisation' + *happy*]

'Demob' here is a shortening of the *demobilisation* of troops that took place at the end of the two world wars. It was in the context of a soldier's rush of excitement at the prospect of being sent home that this expression was first encountered in the post-war era, but in the decades that have followed *demob-happy* has come to be used ever more loosely to refer to a feeling of elation at the prospect of impending release from any unpleasant job or assignment. So if you're feeling a frisson of excitement at the prospect of a festive break from work, you're essentially experiencing *demob-happiness*.

dubbings (*n.*) evergreen branches used as Christmas decorations [1884; ? < *dub*, 'to trim a plant']

Two early and little-used meanings of the word *dub* – to dress, and to trim a plant or hedge – have seemingly become conflated in this curious word.

See also **boun**

filipendulous (*adj.*) hanging or appearing to be hung by a thread [1864; < Lat. *filum*, 'thread' + Lat. *pendulus* 'hanging' + *–ous*]

Whether it's used to describe a festive bauble or decoration on the tree, or just your mental state in the days leading up to Christmas, something that is *filipendulous* is hanging on by the merest of threads.

Gruen Effect (*n.*) the tendency of shoppers to become disoriented in shopping malls [? 1978; < Austrian architect Victor Gruen (1903–80)]

You walk in needing a box of chocolates and some wrapping paper, and walk out three hours later having had lunch and a cappuccino, bought yourself a new pair of jeans and renewed your mobile phone contract. If that sounds familiar (not least in the whirlwind of final shopping days ahead of Christmas), then you can at least take solace in the fact that modern malls and supermarkets are all but designed to make you more susceptible to losing focus, losing track of time, and falling victim to special promotions and impulse purchases.

In the 1970s, Austrian architect Victor Gruen – who had for decades worked in designing retail spaces and shopping malls – publicly decried what he saw as a growing trend among contemporary designers that sought to confuse and overwhelm shoppers, rather than fostering the kind of customer-friendly experience he had always championed. Everything from the size and scale of the modern mall to its cluttered layout, glitzy lighting and reflective surfaces conspires to detach customers from the outside world, thereby making them more prone to forgetting what they went in for, and succumbing to other enticements instead. Although Gruen's name has since become attached to the disorienting 'effect' he described (as well as the so-called 'Gruen transfer' – the moment of forgetfulness at which a shopper loses track of their original plans), Gruen himself was a fierce critic of such designs and the architects responsible for them. So when you're picking out a new set of suitcases or queueing up to watch a movie when all you really need is a pair of socks for your brother-in-law, you can at least be reassured that your lack of focus is not entirely your fault.

holinight (*n.*) an eve, the night before a special day [? 13thC; < *holy* + *night*]

Just as a holiday was originally a 'holy day', a *holinight* was literally a 'holy night' when the word was first recorded in the early Middle English period. It disappeared from the language for several centuries before being unceremoniously resurrected in the 1800s, and has remained on the fringes of our vocabulary as a word for the night before a special event ever since.

holy verd (*n.*) a festive decoration of berry-covered holly boughs [1902; ? < *holly* + *verd*, 'green, greenery']

'Holly used in the Christmas decoration of churches' is how the *English Dialect Dictionary* explained this word in the early 1900s. Etymologically, the 'verd' here likely comes from the same French and Latin roots as *verdant*, but whether the first half of the expression is meant to be *holy*, in apparent reference to its use in churches, or *holly* is unclear.

huckmuck (*n.*) the confusion or frustration that comes from things not being in their right place [dial., 1888; ? < rel. *muck*, 'mess, dirt']

If yours is the kind of home where furniture has to be rearranged and shelves cleared away to make room for a tree, decorations and extra seats around the dining table, then perhaps the week before Christmas has you in something of a *huckmuck*. Recorded in a handful of English dialects dating back to the nineteenth century, *huckmuck* is the confusion caused by everything being thrown into a muddle, and nothing that you need or want being where it usually is.

jowfair (*n.*) something that does not go according to plan, despite much prior preparation [dial., 1896; of unclear origin, ? < *jow*, 'to knock']

'A term applied to anything that does not come off after everything has been prepared' is how the *English Dialect Dictionary* defines this word, before adding the handily disastrous example of 'a wedding, when one of the parties fails to put in an appearance at church'.

Precisely what puts the 'jow' in *jowfair* given that definition is anyone's guess, but there may be some kind of figurative connection to an older verb, *jow* or *jowl*, long used to mean to knock or strike with blows (perhaps in the sense of a party or 'fair' being 'jowed' out of operation). No matter its origin, this is perhaps not a word to focus on as you get everything ready for Christmas, but one nevertheless worth remembering in case things don't quite go to plan . . .

kissing-bunch (*n.*) a kind of festive decoration made of sprigs of mistletoe and other greenery [1877]

Because it remains green throughout the winter – and because it becomes especially visible growing among the branches of trees when all the surrounding leaves have been lost – mistletoe has long been popular at Christmastime, along with its fellow evergreens, holly, ivy and pine. The reason why we kiss beneath it is less easily explained, but for centuries the plant has been associated with new life, regrowth and fertility, and so there is likely meant to be some ancient connection to new love and romance here too. (Not bad for a plant that partly takes its name from *mix*, an Old English word for faecal matter, because its seeds are propagated in the droppings of birds.)

In the nineteenth century, the earlier tradition of using sprigs of mistletoe to decorate the home at Christmastime apparently led to the invention of the *kissing-bunch* or *kissing-bough* – a kind of advent crown affair, consisting of a series of interlocking metal hoops, around which mistletoe and other evergreen sprigs could be wrapped and hung alongside ribbons, paper flowers, apples, oranges and even dolls and effigies of characters from the nativity.

> *This 'kissing-bunch' is always an elaborate affair. The size depends upon the couple of hoops – one thrust through the other – which forms its skeleton. Each of the ribs is garlanded with holly, ivy, and sprigs of other greens, with bits of coloured ribbons and paper roses, rosy-cheeked apples . . . and oranges. Three small dolls are also prepared . . . and these represent our Saviour, the mother of Jesus, and Joseph. . . .* [Mistletoe] *is carefully tied to the bottom of the kissing-bunch, which is then hung in the middle of the house-place.*
>
> *English Dialect Dictionary* (Vol. 3, 1902)

Kissing-bunches were also apparently often hung in the kitchen, by the fireside, or else above the entrance to a room or house – presumably anywhere the most festive footfall beneath it could be guaranteed.

mageiricophobia (*n.*) the fear or dislike of having to cook or prepare food [1965; < Gk. *mageiricos*, 'culinary, skilled in cooking' (< Gk. *mageiros*, 'cook') + *–phobia* (< Gk. *phobos*, 'fear')]

Derived from an ancient Greek word for a cook, if you're dreading the prospect of preparing a Christmas meal for a full house of guests and relatives, then you may well be enduring an anxious bout of *mageiricophobia*.

parasceuological (*adj.*) descriptive of anything done in preparation [1671; partly < Gk. *paraskeue*, 'preparation, procurement']

Parasceuological and its derivatives were originally typically used in relation to religious observances and festivals, before a more general sense emerged in the seventeenth century to give us the perfect term to describe a busy pre-Christmas week of planning and provision.

peggy-work (*n.*) chores, menial household work [naut. sl., 1959; < *peggy*, 'ship's errand-boy']

If the week before Christmas is chock-full of cleaning and tidying, then you have a week of *peggy-work* ahead of you. That's a term from nautical slang, in which a *peggy* is the name given to the member of a ship's crew whose job or whose turn it is to perform some kind of menial or unpleasant chore. Quite where that name comes from in turn is unclear. A large washtub (or else the wooden post used to agitate the laundry inside of it) has been known as a *peggy* since the early 1800s, so there is perhaps meant to be some kind of connection to domestic chores here. Alternatively, as a pet form of the name Margaret, in the eighteenth and nineteenth centuries *Peggy* was commonly used as a jokey nickname for any man who enjoyed cleaning, housework and other tasks that were (at the time, at least) chiefly considered women's work.

pennyworth-o'-Christmas (*n.*) a single sprig or small bunch of festive holly or mistletoe [dial., 1903]

Very much at the 'Bah, humbug' end of the festive decoration scale is a mere *pennyworth-o'-Christmas* – a term likely in use in the nineteenth century for as much festive greenery as a single penny could buy.

powl (*v.*) to leave work early to go to the pub [dial., 1850; of unclear origin]

As the Christmas week goes by, and the festive shutdown of businesses and workplaces becomes imminent, it might feel ever more tempting to go *powlin'* – or 'neglecting work and drinking', as an 1850 guide to *The Dialect of South Lancashire* put it. *Powl* itself, the same book explained, is 'to leave off work and go to the alehouse', while to *powler* is to 'ramble about drinking'. All might seem like good ideas at this time of year.

ramfeezlement (*n.*) the turmoil or confusion caused by trying to do something when you're tired [Sc., 1821; < *ramfeezle*, 'to throw into disarray' (1786, credited to Robert Burns) ? < Sc. *feeze* 'to work non-stop']

'Disorder occasioned by fatigue' is how the *English Dialect Dictionary* defines this word, which might well come in useful when describing the appearance of a Christmas present wrapped well after midnight, or after one too many festive imbibements. Etymologically, it is a derivative of the Scots verb *ramfeezle*, meaning to confuse or throw into disarray, with the initial 'ram–' here apparently used an intensifier to somehow boost or heighten the implication of the word in which appears; other eminently useful Scots words built along similar lines include *ramgunshoch* (bad-tempered), *ramskeerie* (lustful), *ramstageous* (uncouth) and *ramstoorie* (slapdash).

Quite what puts the 'feezle' in *ramfeezlement* is less clear, but there is likely a link to another Scots word, *feeze*. Although it originally meant simply to knot or twist something together with a circular motion, *feeze* later came to be used to mean to work incessantly, apparently an allusive reference to the non-stop circles of a dog's wagging tail.

scuddle (*v.*) to do unpleasant or menial housework in the kitchen [1866; ? < *scudler*, a domestic servant (15thC)]

What exactly constitutes pleasant housework in the kitchen is unclear, but when this word first appeared in the language in the 1500s it merely meant to wash dishes. Over the centuries that followed, the various dialects of English and Scots took that meaning and ran with it, so the regional dictionaries of the nineteenth and early twentieth centuries record this word in a host of more niche meanings, including 'to act as a kitchen-drudge', 'to mess about at domestic work', 'to work in a slatternly way' and – perhaps when all of that becomes too much – 'to wander from home in order to shirk some duty'.

scurryfunge (*v.*) to hastily tidy a house [? 1789; of unclear origin, ? partly < *scour*]

When it first appeared in the language in the late eighteenth century, *scurryfunge* meant both to beat or lash someone, and to scrub something clean (in which case the 'scurry' may be related in some way to *scour*). Aside from the notion of someone moving or working with enough elbow-grease to abrade a surface, how those two meanings are connected (if at all) is a matter of etymological guesswork – as, for that matter, is precisely what a 'funge' is meant to be.

From those murky origins, by the late nineteenth and early twentieth centuries *scurryfunge* appears to have fallen out of use aside from in a handful of regional dialects – most notably in North America, where it was resurrected from relative obscurity in a guide to the dialect of Maine in 1950:

> *Scurryfunge. A hasty tidying of the house between the time you see a neighbor coming and the time she knocks on the door.*
> John Gould, *Maine Lingo* (1950)

See also **thorter**

Tammasmas (*n.*) the evening of the fifth night before Christmas Day, 20–1 December, when it is said to be unlucky to do any work after dusk [Sc., 1899; < *St Thomas's Mass*]

Running out of energy a little ahead of Christmas? Give yourself a break and down tools at dusk on *Tammasmas*, or St Thomas's Mass, in line with an ancient tradition from the Northern Isles of Scotland. Anyone who broke this rule and continued working on the evening of 20 December was supposedly liable to attract bad luck in the days and weeks ahead.

See also **Yules, The**

thorter (*n.*) a quick or slapdash attempt at tidying up [Sc., Ir., 1850; ? < *thwart*]

Thought to be derived from the same root as *thwart*, the word *thorter* has been in use since the fifteenth century in a variety of forms and senses, almost all relating to some way of lying across or 'athwart' something, or else moving in a back-and-forth or up-and-down direction. How that came to be used of the kind of hasty tidy-up (or 'hurried going-over', as the *Scottish National Dictionary* puts it) that we might all be guilty of at this time of year is unclear, but perhaps the image here is meant to be that of a cursory back-and-forth wiping or dusting of a grubby surface – that is, just enough to give the appearance of being clean.

winter-proud (*adj.*) precociously or arrogantly prepared ahead of time [? 19thC]

In literal terms, *winter-proud* is an agricultural term used of wheat or similar plants and crops that, due to unseasonably mild conditions, grow or come into bud too early during the winter. In more figurative terms, however, the word can be used of anyone or anything that appears to act or organise itself precociously ahead of time. So if you're the kind of person for whom the rigours of the Christmas week pose no challenge, then perhaps this is the term to best describe you.

xenodochy (*n.*) hospitality, especially towards strangers [1623; < *xeno–* (< Gk. *xenos*, 'strange') + Gk. *dechomai*, 'to receive']

While *xenophobia* is a dislike of strangers and all things foreign or unfamiliar, *xenodochy* is a wholehearted embrace of them, with the added implication of extended hospitality. And given that Christmas often sees a perilous mix of parents, children and their boyfriends, girlfriends and new partners thrown together, this might be a word worth remembering come Christmas lunchtime.

See also **philoxeny**

young yule (*n.*) the beginning of the festive season, or the start of a holiday period [Sc., 1949]

Yule, as a word for the Christmas period, comes from a Norse word, *jol*, that was originally used of a pagan winter festival, many of whose practices were either adopted into or inspired festive traditions we still observe today. The word *yule* itself crops up in a host of other words and phrases relating to this time of year, many of which make an appearance in this book – including this one. As well as referring to the very beginnings of the Christmas period (or indeed, any period of festivities), *young yule* can be used in a similar way to counting chickens before they're hatched – that is, in reference to a point of time at which it is still too early to know or tell what the outcome of something will be.

Yules, The (*n. pl.*) the seven days before Christmas Day [Sc., ? 19thC]

The pre-Christmas week is an important one in the Northern Isles of Scotland, where this period (or occasionally, the entire month ahead of Christmas) has long been known as *The Yules*. The festivities and rites observed during this time are a hangover from the days when the Vikings ruled the far north of Scotland, and as such are peppered with monsters and superstitions whose origins lie across the sea in Scandinavia.

According to the nineteenth-century Shetland folklorist Jessie Saxby, the Yules began on *Tulya's E'en*, the seventh night before Christmas, when malevolent beings known as trows left the underworld and walked the Earth, supposedly in an attempt to take part in the festive celebrations. The days that followed consisted of various rites intended to see off the threat of the trows, and thereby ensure good health, luck and security for the coming year. So in addition to the observances of **Boo Helly** and **Tammasmas**, the day after Tulya's E'en was Mother's Night, on which it was traditional to recite a blessing over any sleeping children in the household. On Orkney, Sow Day was 17 December, when anyone who kept pigs was expected to slaughter a prize sow in readiness for Christmas Day. And no matter when it fell, the last Sunday before Christmas was known as Byanna's Sunday, or Bainer Sunday, on which it was traditional to serve a boiled cow's head and afterwards set a candle inside the skull ready to be burned on Christmas morning.

yuleshard (*n.*) someone who leaves work unfinished on Christmas Eve [Sc., dial., 1866; < *yule* + *shard* (< *jade*, 'fool, duped person')]

Despite your **charette**, you've decided to **powl**. As a result, you're a *yuleshard*. The 'shard' here is a dialect corruption of the word *jade*, which has been used as a mockingly contemptuous insult since medieval times. If you're 'yule's jade', ultimately, then you're someone who can rightfully be made fun of at Christmastime; oddly, that means that, as well as referring to someone who fails to complete all their work ahead of the Christmas break, this word was also once used of someone who did not receive any new clothes for Christmas and so had to endure the indignity of being seen on the big day by their friends, family and neighbours dressed in clothes that everybody had already seen them in.

> *An opprobrious term for someone who leaves work unfinished before Christmas or the New Year, also for someone who has no new piece of apparel to celebrate the season.*
>
> *Scottish National Dictionary*

9. CHRISTMAS DAY

After weeks of preparation, the big day finally arrives – and with it, ample opportunity to use the words collected in this chapter, which are all to do with friends, family and festivities.

From gift-giving to overindulgence, they round up the best ways to kick back, catch up and make the most of Christmas Day.

angel visit (*n.*) a pleasurable but fleeting event or visitation [1799]

An allusive and appropriately festive reference to the miraculous appearance of angels, *angel visit* has been used metaphorically since the eighteenth century of any pleasurable event or long-awaited visit that feels all too short and occurs all too infrequently. As much as this could refer to Christmas Day itself, if you're heading home for the holidays – or have friends and relatives you now tend only to see at Christmases and birthdays – the term could well be applied to the festive catch-ups with much-loved people that likewise feel all too few and far between.

antipelargy (*n.*) the love felt mutually between members of a family [1649, Gk. *anti*–, 'resembling' + Gk. *pelargos*, 'stork']

Storks have long been considered intensely protective and affectionate birds, with one quirk of ancient folklore suggesting stork parents were so willing to do whatever was necessary to raise their young that they would even rear them on their own blood. Thanks to long-standing (if fairly macabre) myths like this, the curious word *antipelargy* literally means 'resembling a stork'. Much on display during the festive season, *antipelargy* is the kind of reciprocal, mutual love and affection that exists naturally between family members – and particularly between parents and their children.

belly-cheer (*n.*) gluttonous feasting [1549]

'The gratification of the belly' is how the first edition of the *Oxford English Dictionary* defined this Tudor-period coinage way back in 1887. Feel free to use this as a verb too, meaning 'to feast luxuriously'.

belsnickel (*v.*) to go Christmas merrymaking [1881; < *Belsnickel*, name of a folkloric character]

A figure from traditional German (and now parts of North American) folklore, Belsnickel is the name of a peculiar gift-giving associate of St Nicholas, often depicted as an older man with a long dark beard, dressed in dirty, raggedy furs and holding a hessian sack full of presents slung over his back. Originating in southern Germany, the character was taken to the USA by German immigrants in the late 1700s and early 1800s, and it was there that his name eventually became a verb: to go *belsnickeling* is to go about merrymaking at Christmastime, often by calling upon friends and neighbours to hand out gifts, sing carols and comic songs, and to play festive games and pranks. In return, the merrymakers can expect small gifts and tokens from their hosts, as well as seasonal food and drinks for their efforts.

bishop (*n.*) the molten ring or ridge of wax that forms around the flame of a burning candle [1611; < *bishop*, 'high-ranking clergyman']

Candles have long been associated with Christmastime. The age-old tradition of lighting a candle on either Christmas Eve or

Christmas morning might even date back to a time when it was still considered a pagan festival, and the light and heat from the candle's flame were intended to ward off ill luck and malevolent spirits. Different faiths and cultures have their own versions and interpretations of the Christmas candle too, of course, with one popular Christian tradition suggesting that the light is meant to represent the Star of Bethlehem, guiding the Wise Men to the birth of Jesus. Even folklore gets in on the act: an old Irish tradition has it that a family should light twelve rush candles on Twelfth Night, 6 January; whoever's candle burns the longest is destined to be the longest lived.

Given that they play such a significant part in Christmas culture, it is perhaps understandable that candles have a vocabulary all of their own. The burned and blackened part of the candlewick is called the *snaste*. The tiny spike in the bottom of a candlestick that holds the candle in place is called the *pricket*. And once a candle has been lit, the small molten hollow of liquid wax that often forms around the flame is known as the *bishop*.

Quite where this name comes from is a mystery, but bishops have long endured a rather unwelcome reputation for pious hypocrisy: forked signposts or 'fingerposts' that point the direction of travel from a roadside were once scurrilously known as *bishop's fingers* because although they showed the right way to go, they never actually went that way themselves. Ultimately, it has been suggested that, sometime around the early seventeenth century, the ring of wax around a candle became known as the *bishop* because despite its proximity to the light and heat of the flame, it remained far enough away not to be consumed by it.

catillate (*v.*) to lick a plate clean [1623; < Lat. *catillus*, 'dish']

A word quite literally to savour. Derived from a Latin word for a small plate or dish, *catillate* (like the previous entry here) was first recorded in Henry Cockeram's *English Dictionarie* back in the early 1600s.

cicisbeo (*n.*) a decorative knot of ribbon [1700s; < It., of unknown origin]

In its more usual sense, a *cicisbeo* is the young lover or handsome gallant of a married high-society lady, who with the full consent and cooperation of her husband is permitted to attend public and social occasions by her side. The word's origins are as questionable as the relationship it describes, with different theories ranging from an Italian or French pet name literally meaning 'little chickpea' to an onomatopoeic suggestion that the word is meant to replicate the whispers that would no doubt follow the pair wherever they went.

What is more reliably known is that in the later eighteenth century, *cicisbeo* gained a somewhat unexpected additional meaning, coming to refer to a decorative knot of ribbon. As tempting as it is to presume this might have emerged figuratively, implying that the woman's *cicisbeo* was a mere social adornment, the connection is a more obvious one: following the style at the time, fashionable young men would often wear ribbons as part of their costume, or else tie decorative knots or trailing garlands of ribbon to their walking canes or swords.

colliby (*n.*) a small present [15thC; ? < Lat. *collybus*, 'cash exchange']

Derived from an ancient Greek word for a small coin, in Latin a *collybus* was an exchange of money, or a trading of different currencies, which makes a *collybist* a usurer or money-lender. It may be that *colliby* comes directly from there, and in its original medieval context perhaps implied not just a small gift, but a gift or tip of cash or **present-silver**. More likely, however, is that somewhere along the line this word became confused with a different Latin root, *collibere*, meaning to please or make happy, and ultimately came to imply not just cash, but a little present of any kind given merely to lift the recipient's spirits. (Though the cash would be just fine too, let's be honest.)

confelicity (*n.*) joy in other people's happiness [1900; < *con–*, 'together' + Lat. *felicitas*, 'happiness']

Considering how familiar and well-used the word *schadenfreude* is to describe the malicious relishing of another's downfall or misfortune, it speaks volumes that this term for its direct opposite is so unfamiliar. In fact, it has scarcely been used in the century or so since it was apparently first introduced by the American psychologist G. Stanley Hall in 1900, alongside its German equivalent, *mitfreude*.

congiary (*n.*) a gift intended to be shared or divided among a group of people [1601; < Lat. *congius*, 'vessel']

In the Roman world, a *congius* was a kind of vessel used as a measure of capacity, equivalent to around 6 or 7 pints. It was often the case that the contents of the congius (typically wine or ale, or some valuable commodity like corn or salt) were intended to be shared among a group, particularly of soldiers, and it is from there that an English equivalent, *congiary*, fell into use in the language in the early seventeenth century. Although typically used only in reference to the communal gifts of ancient Rome (and still a vanishingly rare word at the best of times), there is little reason why it should not be brought back into use in the season of goodwill and gift-giving today.

cosaque (*n.*) a Christmas cracker [1858 < Fr., lit. 'Cossack']

When Christmas crackers first went on sale in Victorian England in the mid 1800s, one of the names under which they were sold was *cosaques*, the French word for 'Cossacks', supposedly in playful reference to the cracking gunfire of Russian Cossack soldiers. The very earliest Christmas crackers, however, were known as *cracker bon-bons*, as they typically comprised nothing more than a small parcel of sweet treats, twisted shut at both ends, that split with a bang when pulled apart.

crawmassing (*n.*) gathering up festive leftovers [dial., 1877; ? < *comassing*, 'begging favours' (< *commerce*, 'exchange')]

Related to an earlier word, *comassing*, for begging or asking favours from friends and neighbours, *crawmassing* came to refer specifically to 'gathering up the remains of a feast' at Christmastime. Although the origins of both words are decidedly hazy, in the sense of somehow seeking out a deal or exchange it has been suggested they may ultimately be dialect alterations of *commerce*.

dolce-far-nientism (*n.*) a determination to do absolutely nothing and unapologetically enjoy it; the state of being happily idle [1860, < It. *dolce far niente*, 'sweet doing nothing']

The Italian expression *dolce far niente* was borrowed into English in the early 1800s to describe the sheer delight taken in doing absolutely nothing; in its native language, it literally means 'sweet to do nothing'. The fairly jokey invention *dolce-far-nientism* followed a few decades later to describe the state of doing – or a resolute determination to do – nothing at all (and to be very happy and unapologetic about it). In other words, this is a word well worth bearing in mind for the inevitable post-lunch snooze on Christmas afternoon.

donatory (*n.*) the recipient of a gift [1617; < Lat. *donatorius*, 'recipient']

If a gift-giver is a *donor* or *donator*, then the gift-receiver is the *donee* or *donatory*. All four of these words derive ultimately from the Latin *donare*, meaning to give or bestow – which in etymological terms also puts the 'don' in *pardon* and *condone*.

doniferous (*adj.*) bearing or carrying a gift [1656; partly < Lat. *donum*, 'gift' (< Lat. *donare*, 'to give')]

Whether it's the guests turning up at your door on Christmas morning, or the colleagues at the office party getting ready to swap their Secret Santas, there are plenty of *doniferous* people around at this time of year. Like the previous entry here, this word derives from the Latin *donare*, meaning to give, plus *ferre*, another Latin word meaning to bear or carry (which as well as putting the 'fer' in words like *transfer* and *vociferous*, is also the origin of the literally 'cone-bearing' *conifer* tree).

eucharistia (*n.*) a statement or expression of thanks on receiving a gift [1593; < Gk. lit. 'thanksgiving']

Eucharistia is the Greek word for a thanksgiving, but in the language of rhetoric and literary eloquence it has come to be used of any turn of phrase that acts as an expression of gratitude. Unsurprisingly, this root too is the etymological origin of the Christian *Eucharist*.

eudaemonics (*n. pl.*) **pleasures, things that make you happy [1832; < Gk.** ***eudaimonia*****, 'happiness']**

While the adjective *eudaemonic* can be used to describe anything that is conducive to happiness, it was the philosopher Jeremy Bentham who first used it as a noun in English, defining *eudaemonics* as 'the art of applying life to the maximisation of wellbeing' in 1832. Later writers have twisted Bentham's idea of the word, giving us a more general term for anything that makes you happy – be that material things lying in wait under the Christmas tree, or the more spiritual **confelicity** of the festive season.

excuse-us (*n.*) **a gift given to a host in recognition of hospitality [1938]**

If your Christmas period involves taking care of houseguests or else bedding down in a parent or relative's spare room for the holidays, then an *excuse-us* – a term first popularised in 1930s America – may well be on the cards.

fairing (*n.*) **a small gift or trinket, especially one bought at a fair or by a lover [1574; <** ***fair*****, 'fete, festival']**

Dating back to Tudor times, a *fairing* was originally any small trinket or souvenir purchased at a country fair. By the late 1500s and early 1600s, however, a more specific meaning had emerged in that language that turned a *fairing* into any such small gift purchased and presented to you by a lover or sweetheart.

fictive kin (*n.*) the network of friends and non-blood relatives who are considered members of a family [? early 20thC; < *fictive*, 'fictional, not genuine']

Christmas is a time for family and friends, but in the modern world those two groups are often blurred, and what we consider to be our family now stretches far beyond the usual bounds of our blood relatives. The indispensable network of friends and non-blood relatives who surround a family so closely that they are considered members of it – to the extent that younger members often know them as aunts and uncles, despite there being no actual family ties – is its *fictive kin*. The adjective *fictive* literally means fictional, imaginary or counterfeit, but there is nothing feigned or fanciful about the ties that bind these much-loved outside members to a family unit.

finifugal (*adj.*) avoiding or shunning the completion of something, not wanting something to end [1883; < Lat. *finis*, 'end' + *fuga*, 'flight']

Merry old souls who don't want the festive cheer to come to an end at Christmastime may benefit from this obscure and vanishingly rare adjective from the late 1800s. Derived from Latin roots essentially meaning a 'fleeing from the end', this is the perfect word for those of us who wish the Christmas spirit could last the whole year round.

frilal (*n.*) an ornamental border of ribbons [17thC; partly ? < *frill*]

A word worth remembering if you like to go all-out in your present wrapping, *frilal* is likely a combination of the earlier and more familiar word *frill* alongside the rather less well-known *fal-lal*, a centuries-old term for a showy but ultimately throwaway adornment or frippery.

fructure (*n.*) the use or enjoyment of the fruits of your labour [1611; < Lat. *fructus*, 'enjoyment']

After weeks of organisation, Christmas Day is the time, at long last, to sit back and enjoy the spoils of all your hard work – or to make the most of the *fructure* of your efforts.

gersum (*n.*) an especially costly or treasured gift [OE; lit. 'gift']

If you've heard of this word before, this likely wasn't the meaning you were anticipating here. That's because in legal parlance a *gersum*, or *garsom*, is a fine expected to be paid as a forfeit by someone who enters or strays onto another person's land or property. The word has been in use in that sense since medieval times, but before then – back in the very early days of Old English – a *gersum* was merely any especially treasured item or possession or, by extension, a particularly costly gift.

hearthmuster (*n.*) a circle of friends or family gathered around a fireside [dial., 1876; < *hearth* + *muster*, 'a calling together, a gathering']

It seems ironic that the warm-hearted reunions and family get-togethers of Christmas happen at the coldest and bleakest time of the year. If you are nevertheless able to meet up with friends and family despite the elements, then you might find yourselves huddled together with a warm drink in hand, by an equally warming fire – in which case your festive reunion has become a *hearthmuster*. A Yorkshire dialect word recorded from the second half of the nineteenth century, it refers to a 'family circle at the fireside', according to one 1876 definition.

See also **jamb-friends**

jamb-friends (*n.*) good friends with whom to relax around a fireside [1877; < *jamb*, 'upright timber' + *friends*]

Once you're installed somewhere suitably **howffy**, what could be better than surrounding yourself with *jamb-friends*? The *jamb* here is the upright supporting timber of a fireplace, which makes your *jamb-friends* just the kind of good, close friends with whom you would happily spend an evening relaxing by a fireside.

See also **hearthmuster**

joblijock (*n.*) anything that disturbs the peace and comfort of home [dial., 1868; < earlier *joblijock*, 'male turkey, rooster']

'A smoking chimney' or 'a scolding wife' are the two examples of *joblijocks* given in an 1868 *Glossary of the Cleveland Dialect*, which defines this word as anything that tends to 'interfere with domestic comfort or peace'. Come Christmastime, that could mean the overexcitement of kids, the sound of their newest toys, or just Christmas itself and all the upheaval and uproar it can bring with it.

In suitably festive fashion too, *joblijock* was originally a word for a male turkey (invented onomatopoeically in imitation of its gobbling call); it likely came to refer to an unwelcome disturber of the local peace in reference to the early-morning calls of roosters.

kedge-gutted (*adj.*) made to feel sick through overeating [dial., ? 1889; < *kedge*, 'protruding stomach']

The *kedge* is the stomach or a protruding belly, which means that someone who is *kedgy* is 'given to the pleasures of the table', in the words of the *English Dialect Dictionary*. Someone or something described as *kedge-gutted*, meanwhile, has eaten sufficient to make themselves feel ill, making this an optimal word for Christmas afternoon (or, should there be a lot of leftovers, Boxing Day lunchtime).

kirsmas-glass (*n.*) a festive toast [dial., 1898; lit. 'Christmas glass']

'A glass of liquor drunk to wish success to the house on Christmas Day' is a *kirsmas-glass*, according to the *English Dialect Dictionary*, which pinpoints this curious expression to the Lakeland region of the English northwest.

knee-buckles (*n.*) a useless gift [? 18thC]

'Like knee-buckles to a Highlander!' goes an old Irish expression, implying that something (or someone, should the context demand it) is utterly and completely useless. As was the style in the eighteenth century, men would often use ornate buckles to fasten and secure their breeches and hose at the knee. But because Highlanders wore kilts, they had no need for such frippery and hence the term came to be used of any similarly redundant or useless item.

laetification (*n.*) joyful rejoicing, festive merrymaking [1485; < Lat. *laetificare*, 'to make glad' (< Lat. *laetus*, 'joyful')]

You're not just enjoying yourself on Christmas Day, you're *laetificating*. Adapted from a Latin word meaning joyful or gladdened, *laetification* fell into use in English in the fifteenth century, followed by the related verb, *laetificate* ('to enjoy') a century later, and the adjective *laetificant* ('gladdening, spirit-lifting') in the mid 1600s. As well as describing anything that makes a person feel cheerful or festive, *laetificant* was also used in medical contexts to refer to the stimulating or uplifting effects of certain tonics and preparations – a draft of which you might well need to lift yourself back up after Christmas dinner.

largition (*n.*) the generous bestowal of gifts [*c.* 1475; < Lat. *largiri*, 'to give generously']

In terms of generosity, *largition* is an etymological cousin of *largesse* – and just like its cousin, it can be also used to refer to gifts so generously bestowed that an implication of bribery or coercion may lie not far behind it. So if you're trying to win someone over with something you've placed under the tree (or you fear someone may be trying to coerce you with something placed there for you), then this term may well come in useful on Christmas morning.

lucky-bird (*n.*) the first person to cross the threshold of your home on Christmas morning [1862]

In some parts of England, it was (and still is) tradition to officially 'let Christmas in' on Christmas morning. Quite what this particular festive rigmarole entails differs from county to county, and often from one town or village to the next. But typically it involves ensuring that a dark-haired man or young boy is the first person invited into your home on the morning of Christmas Day, so long as he has had the foresight to bring with him some suitable festive token – in some regions a sweet pie or biscuit, in others a draft of drink or a sprig of holly or fir.

For reasons that have long since been lost to the mists of folkloric time, this festive first-footer is known as the *lucky-bird*, and is rewarded for his efforts by the head of the household with a gift of food and drink, as well as a small amount of cash or some other suitably tokenish present.

> *If the duty of 'letting Christmas in' has not fallen to the lot of some other individual by pre-arrangement, which is generally the case, the lad is admitted, who brings along with him a twig or leaf of evergreen and leaves it behind him, as he is the first-comer, or 'lucky-bird'. He then receives bread and cheese and always money . . . Upon no account whatever is a female allowed to step over the threshold first. A more unlucky event than this could not well be . . . and chiefly for this reason, the door is kept secured till Christmas has been duly 'let in'.*
>
> C. Clough Robinson, *The Dialect of Leeds and Its Neighbourhood* (1862)

The traditional rules surrounding the lucky-bird's entrance into a home are as varied as they are unusual. In many regions, redheads are given the same injunction at Christmas as they are for the New Year's **qualtagh** celebrations. In others, local folklore demands a bachelor or a singleton be preferred over someone who is betrothed, married or widowed. Because parents with young children obviously need another reason to get out of bed early on Christmas morning, in some parts of the country the entire lucky-bird ritual takes place just after dawn. And perhaps most bizarre of all, in rural Northumberland tradition demands the lucky-bird not be flat-footed, but be someone with a high arch and instep – the acid test of suitability apparently being someone beneath whose foot a stream of water can flow unimpeded.

mathom (*n.*) a precious trinket, given as a gift; a little throwaway item [OE; 'valuable, treasure']

A word with a somewhat unusual history, a *mathom* in early Old English was an especially valued gift or item of treasure. It fell by the linguistic wayside sometime around the thirteenth century and would likely have remained a long-forgotten relic were it not for J. R. R. Tolkien, who resurrected the word in *The Lord of the Rings* in 1954 – this time with the slightly tweaked meaning of a rather less valued item of bric-a-brac.

misportion (*v.*) to make yourself ill by overeating [Sc., 1808; < *mis–*, 'bad, wrong' + *portion*]

The implication in this word is that you have either been given or have given yourself a misguidedly oversized portion of food. But then again, if you're not doing that on Christmas Day, are you really doing Christmas Day properly?

oblation (*n.*) the act of bestowing a gift [15thC; < Lat. *oblatio*, 'offering']

Oblation began life as a religious term referring to the act of offering something to God or to the church. That meaning still survives in ecclesiastic contexts, but since the 1400s *oblation* has also been used in a more general sense for the act of offering or bestowing any gift, no matter what and no matter on whom.

overquat (*v.*) to eat too much food [13thC; < *over–* + ME *quat*, 'to satisfy']

If you are *quatted*, or *quotted*, then you're fully satiated or glutted, so to *overquat* is to eat past the point of fullness. Fittingly, the verb *quat* can also be used to mean to crouch down, or to sit or lie as low as possible, which may well be the only way you can get comfortable after a period of bloated overindulgence.

pang (*v.*) to force an unwanted gift or item onto someone [Sc., dial., 1894; of unknown origin]

Before there was regifting, there was *panging*. In this context, *pang* began life as an eighteenth-century word meaning to pack or cram something full, and it was in the sense of a forceful push that, around the turn of the last century, it came to be used of the act of palming something unwanted or unpleasant onto someone else. 'The man panged this poor cheese on us' was the example sentence given by a *Dictionary of Northumberland Words* way back in 1894. Regifting, it seems, is nothing new.

pea for a bean, to give a (*v. phr.*) to give a small gift with an eye to receiving a better or larger one in return [? 18thC; < Fr.]

This is a literal English translation of an earlier French saying, *donner un pois pour avoir une fève*, which as well as meaning to give something in the hope of receiving something better in return was (unlike in English) apparently also used of tit-for-tat exchanges, in which one thing was equally matched to another. As well as swapping peas for beans, other versions of this saying refer to giving bread for gingerbread, and baiting a fishing rod with a sprat to catch a mackerel.

present-silver (*n.*) money given in lieu of a gift [14thC]

Also known as *presentation silver*, this term can additionally be used of money given to a gift-giver as a means of recompense or an expression of thanks. The sense given above is the older one, though, in use since the mid fourteenth century at least.

ramracketting (*n.*) Christmas gambolling [1777; ? < rel. *racket*, 'loud noise, disturbance']

As well as being used of a noisy rabble of rural villagers (or a 'country rout', in the words of the *English Dialect Dictionary*), *ramracketting* is an eighteenth-century West Country word for what one writer at the time described as 'Christmas gambols, where all is capering and dancing, noise and rattling'. Quite what was causing the 'rattling', and exactly what the enigmatic 'capering' involved, are both unfortunately unclear – as, for that matter, are this curious word's origins.

The *English Dialect Dictionary* also notes *rammack* as a local word meaning 'to rush about riotously', so *ramracket* may just be a playful extension of that. Alternatively, the root here might be a noisy *racket*, with the prefix *ram–* somehow meant to emphasise the noise and commotion involved. No matter its pedigree or its practice, however, *ramracketting* is still a word worth reviving if your Christmas Day 'gambols' turn similarly boisterous.

reciproque (*n.*) something mutually given and received; a gift given in return to someone who has given you something [1536; < Fr. *réciproque*, 'reciprocal' (< Lat.)]

As an adjective, *reciproque* just means reciprocal or mutual, but since the 1500s it has also been used as a noun to refer to something given in return, or as part of a fair or identical exchange.

regalo (*n.*) a gift of expensive food or drink [1622; ? < Sp. or It., 'gift']

Borrowed into English in the seventeenth century, a *regalo* can be both a lavish gift of food or drink, and an equally lavish party or entertainment. Either way it's a word well suited to the gift-giving season.

rere-supper (*n.*) a second supper, a final snack before bedtime [14thC; ME *rere–*, 'rear, at the back' + *supper*]

If Christmas evening draws in and you've still not eaten your fill, there will no doubt be leftovers knocking around the kitchen – or if you're lucky, a cheeseboard yet to be broken into – just in time for your *rere-supper*.

réveillon (*n.*) a celebratory feast held in the early hours of Christmas morning [1766; < Fr., ultimately < *réveiller*, 'to wake']

Rooted in a French word meaning to wake up, in the sixteenth century a *réveillon* was merely a night-time meal. In the 1700s, however, that meaning narrowed and the word came to refer more specifically to a meal eaten after mass on Christmas Eve night, or in the early hours after the celebrations of New Year's Day.

superstitious pie (*n.*) a Christmas mince pie [*c.* 1698]

This bizarre name arose in the seventeenth century among Puritans who wanted to eat festive mince pies without appearing to condone the festivities themselves. Calling them by this name seemingly freed them from any accusations of double standards, allowing them to enjoy the pies in peace while separating themselves from the festival they abhorred.

swage (*v.*) to relax after a large meal [18thC; < earlier ME *swage*, 'to calm, to mitigate']

A none-too-distant relative of *assuage*, to *swage* or *swadge* originally meant merely to relieve or make better when it first appeared in medieval English more than six centuries ago. The far more specific use of the word in relation to digesting food was a later development that emerged in the eighteenth century. It survives in Scots and a handful of English dialects today.

toe-cover (*n.*) an inexpensive but ultimately useless gift [1948; of unknown origin]

Is this a jokey reference to the last-minute habit of buying everyone new socks for Christmas? Perhaps, though the definitive story of this curious expression's origin is sadly lacking.

toom-handed (*adj.*) bringing or carrying nothing, bearing no gift [Sc., 1896; < OE *tom*, 'empty']

Derived from an Old English word meaning empty or vacant, the expression *toom-handed* had long meant simply empty-handed before, in the late nineteenth century, the *Scottish National Dictionary* noted the more specific use in reference to failing to turn up somewhere with a gift.

vinipote (*n.*) a wine drinker [1623; < Lat. *vinum*, 'wine' + Lat. *potus*, 'drink, drinking' (< Lat. *potare*, 'to drink')]

vinolent (*adj.*) **fond of drinking wine; tending to drink wine to the point of drunkenness [14thC; < Lat.** ***vīnolentus*****, 'having drunk wine, intoxicated' (< Lat.** ***vinum*****, 'wine' + Lat.** ***–olentus*****, suffix implying 'abounding in, full of']**

vinomadefied (*adj.*) **soaked in wine [1652; < Lat.** ***vinum*****, 'wine' + Lat.** ***madefieri*****, 'to make wet']**

A trio of wine words, all derived ultimately from *vinum*, the Latin for wine, for the festive cork-poppers amongst us.

wait-song (*n.*) **a Christmas carol, a piece of festive music [1872; <** ***wait*****, 'local band of musicians']**

From medieval times it was long par for the course for many English towns and villages to have an official band of civic musicians, known as *waits*. The duties of the waits were many and varied, and largely depended on the size of the community in which they played and the number of players there were in the town. But everything from playing in the street and waking people up to performing fanfares and anthems to announce civic dignitaries and royal visits could fall under their remit.

Once common all over the country, by the eighteenth and nineteenth centuries waits were becoming ever rarer, until eventually they largely disappeared altogether – save for at Christmastime. No longer official musicians hired for civic and ceremonial duties, so-called *Christmas waits* were bands of volunteer or amateur musicians and carollers who would perform suitably festive tunes and melodies for the entertainment of the local people. And a *wait-song* was precisely one of those.

wanthrift (*n.*) someone who lacks economy and spends lavishly [1586; < *want*, 'to lack' + *thrift*, 'frugality, economy']

If your largesse and **largition** know no bounds at Christmastime, then perhaps you're a *wanthrift*. Should that term not strike quite the right chord with you, not to worry – the dictionary is just as uneconomical when it comes to words for uneconomical people, as a wasteful and spendthrift person can also be known as a *fool-large* (1400s), a *scapethrift* (1500s), a *stroy-good* (1540), a *spend-all* (1553), a *dingthrift* (1566), a *scattergood* (1577), a *dangwallet* (1826), a *little-thrift* (1849) and, in wartime parlance at least, a *squander-bug* (1943).

whullup (*v.*) to coax or attempt to curry favour with someone by offering them a gift [1808; ? < Sc. *whully*, 'to dupe']

German has a superb word, *drachenfutter*, for a gift offered by a husband in an attempt to placate his wife; rather evocatively, it literally means 'dragon-fodder'. The approximate Scots equivalent *whullup* perhaps isn't quite so evocative, but according to the nineteenth-century Scottish lexicographer John Jamieson it describes the act of currying favour with someone, with the added implication of 'bestowing a small gift on the person whose good graces are courted'.

wonderclout (*n.*) something showy but ultimately worthless [1570; < *wonder* + ? *clout*, 'a blow, a hit']

When this word first appeared in the sixteenth century, it was used of babbling, blathering language that seemed impressive but carried little meaning. The implication of something promising much but delivering nothing caught on, however, and *wonderclout* soon became a more general term for something that looks good but is ultimately worthless – essentially, an Elizabethan stocking-filler.

A *clout* is a stout knock or blow, so perhaps the implication of this word is something that is literally 'striking', but ultimately unwanted or unwelcome. That being said, in the sense of only giving the appearance of something impressive, the history of this word may well be intertwined with an even earlier Tudor example, a *man* or *king of clouts*, for a clownish entertainer dressed as a king – or, metaphorically, a pompous buffoon elevated to high standing. And you can provide your own examples of that.

xenium (*n.*) a gift given to a stranger or houseguest [18thC; < Gk. *xenion*, 'gift (of food) given by a host to a guest' (< Gk. *xenos*, 'strange')]

Just like **xenodochy** before it, *xenium* has its roots in the Greek word *xenos*, meaning strange. In antiquity, a *xenium* typically took the form of a lavish table of treats and delicacies of which a guest could eat their fill.

Yorkshire compliment (*n.*) a gift given thoughtlessly and received unwillingly [1864]

With apologies to everyone from God's Own Country, this nineteenth-century turn of phrase is apparently yet another reference to the stereotypical (and wholly unjustified) reputation of Yorkshire people as skinflints. In the words of a 1904 dictionary of *Slang and its Analogues*, a *Yorkshire compliment* is 'a gift useless to the giver, and not wanted by the receiver'.

yule-girth (*n.*) the peacefulness of Christmastime [1569; < *yule* + *girth* (< OE, ON *grith*, 'peace')]

Despite all the shopping, the decorating, the partying, the last-minute rush to have everything prepared, plus the excitement of Christmas Eve and Christmas morning, there is still a unique kind of quietude to the Christmas period. Businesses shut down, shops remain closed, the streets and roads fall quiet, and on a peaceful Christmas morning it can seem like the entire world has (albeit temporarily) come to a halt. And there is a word for precisely this moment of festive tranquillity: *yule-girth*.

Derived from Norse, *grith* (or, as it later became, *girth*) was an Old English word variously used to mean peace, security, protection or (in the sense of a temporary pause in hostilities) a truce. A *girth-gate*, meanwhile, was a road or route known to provide safe travel. A *girth-stone* was a stone marking the edge of a churchyard, and ultimately used as a sign of sanctuary or asylum. And *yule-girth* was the temporary cessation of all legal procedures over the festive period. It was likely this latter legal pause in proceedings that inspired the use of *yule-girth* as another word for the general serenity and quietude of Christmas, which was first recorded in the 1500s. Sadly, as much as this word has stood the test of time, the festive peacefulness it describes is often all too short-lived.

yule-gut (*n.*) an oversized stomach, caused by eating and drinking too much at Christmas [1656]

A word from the seventeenth century, proving that festive gluttony is by no means anything new.

yule-hole (*n.*) the hole to which a belt is moved after eating too much at Christmastime [Sc., 1736]

'The bag to the auld stent, and the belt to the Yule hole' was the eighteenth-century proverb in which this word was first recorded. The *bag*, in this instance, is the stomach, while a *stent* is a great extent; put together, this saying was used of anyone who appeared as hungry as someone sitting down to Christmas lunch, with their belt loosened in preparation for a good feed.

yule-starn (*n.*) an especially or noticeably bright star in the Christmas Eve sky [Sc., dial., 1886; < *yule* + *starn*, 'star']

Starn is simply an old word for a star, which still survives in a handful of dialects and regions, as well as in quaint phrases like *starnshot* (a shooting-star) and *starnlight* (a flashing in the eyes, as might be caused by a blow to the head). A *yule-starn*, ultimately, is just a Christmas star – or rather, a particularly bright or noticeable star in the sky on Christmas night.

zwodder (*n.*) a period of mental and physical drowsiness [dial., 1825; ? < OE *swother*, 'to slumber']

A busy week combined with an early start to the day and far, far too much food and drink might all conspire on Christmas afternoon to you slipping comfortably into a slumbering *zwodder* – a term from the West Country for what the *English Dialect Dictionary* calls 'a drowsy, stupid state of body or mind'.

10. THE NEW YEAR

Just as the champagne corks stop popping and your head begins to clear after Christmas, you remember there is still one more celebratory night ahead as the year finally comes to an end.

Historically, the new year was seen as a time for making fresh starts, giving people an opportunity to say goodbye to the woes of the previous twelve months and look ahead to better fortune in the year ahead. As a result, many of the words that came to be associated with the new year period are rooted in local good-luck traditions and superstitious folklore, but there are words in this collection too relating to gifts, promises and New Year's resolutions.

Altogether now, 10 . . . 9 . . . 8 . . .

apophoret (*n.*) a gift given at New Year [1623; < Lat. *apophoretum* (< Gk. *apopherein*, 'to carry away')]

Despite its obvious usefulness as a word for the customary bottle of wine you take to a host's house at New Year, this curious term popped up in a handful of dictionaries in the early 1600s, seemingly never caught on, and fell by the linguistic wayside a century or so later. Although some definitions labelled it as simply another word for a present of any kind, the specific reference to a gift given at New Year was recorded first – though quite where it comes from is unclear, as the word itself literally means 'a thing carried away'.

Boxing Time (*n.*) the time between Christmas Day and the end of the first week of January [1831; < Boxing Day]

Boxing Day, 26 December, takes its name from an old tradition in which workers or shop-owners would receive Christmas boxes as gifts from their employers or customers after their businesses reopened the day after Christmas. By the early nineteenth century, this gift-swapping period had apparently been extended through the entire post-Christmas period, known as Boxing Time, which lasted well into the first week of January.

> *Boxing-time, during which Christmas boxes or gratuities are given to servants and dependants . . . begins on the first week-day after Christmas Day, and continues until Epiphany.*
>
> *Nelson's Encyclopedia* (1907)

cockstride (*n.*) a short or insignificant distance; proverbially, the length of time by which the days grow longer after New Year [1626; < *cock*, 'cockerel' + *stride*, 'single pace']

It's fair to say chickens don't have the longest of legs in the animal kingdom, and hence a *cockstride* has been a proverbially insignificant distance since the early seventeenth century at least. As well as being the length by which the days are gradually said to extend in the new year ('At twelf-day the days are lengthened a cock-stride', as one proverb put it back in 1678), *cockstrides* also once formed the basis of a host of other titbits of rustic knowledge and folklore: it was believed, for example, that a lost or unquiet spirit could be silenced by allowing it to return to its home, but only by a distance of one cockstride per year.

étrenne (*n.*) a New Year gift [1760; < Fr. (< Lat. *strenae*, 'festive gifts')]

In ancient Rome, a ritual took place on 1 January each year in which twigs were cut from a small grove in the city dedicated to Strenua, the Roman goddess of the new year, and carried to the citadel in time for the arrival of the newly elected city consuls. This ritual later inspired a more general tradition of handing out New Year gifts – known as *strenae*, taken from Strenua's name – as tokens of good luck and good fortune. In French, the Latin *strenae* gradually turned into *étrenne*, before the word fell into use in English in the early 1700s.

fedifraction (*n.*) the breaking of an oath or promise [1650; < Lat. *fedus*, 'treaty, covenant' + *–fraction* (< Lat. *frangere*, 'to break')]

See **pollicitation**

handsel (*n.*) a New Year's gift; a gift given to the first person to do something, or to wish good luck to someone starting a new endeavour [OE; < OE *hand* + *selen*, 'to give over']

Handsel was originally a rather general Old English term for the act of giving or literally 'handing' something over to someone, but by the Middle English period it had begun to be used more figuratively to refer to omens and prophesising signs – literal 'gifts' from above, taken as signals that something momentous was destined to occur. Now tinged with superstition, the word soon started to be used to refer to the act of giving someone something as a sign or wish of good luck and, in particular at the beginning of the year, as a means of guaranteeing good fortune for the months ahead.

As the word was passed down over the centuries, it continued to pick up a raft of similar meanings referring to some manner of beginning or fresh start. In that sense, as well as the other meanings outlined here, a *handsel* can be the first instalment of a payment or bond, a gift given at the commencement of a new job or a new stage of life, the first use of something newly bought or acquired, the first fruits of someone's labour, a morning's earnings or takings in a business, and even the first customer or first sale made after opening business first thing in the morning.

hearthstone talk (*n.*) boastful chatter; promises made in the evening that are not intended to be followed through, or are immediately broken, the following morning [1875]

Even without the pressure of coming up with a resolution, there's something about New Year's Eve that brings out the great forward-planner in us all. The year's watershed moment suddenly (after a drink or two, at least) seems like the perfect time to set yourself new goals and challenges, which – this year, *definitely* this year – you are absolutely determined to achieve. Then, of course, the drinks keep flowing, the champagne corks keep popping and all those grand promises seem just a little *too* grand in the cold light of New Year's morning. In the end, it was all mere *hearthstone talk* – that is, empty bluster and boastfulness: perhaps the New Year's equivalent of fireside **pokertalk**.

matutinal (*adj.*) getting up early, feeling fresh in the morning [1834; < Lat. *Mater Matuta*, Roman goddess of the morning]

Waking up fresh and active on the morning of 1 January tends to depend on what you were doing on 31 December, of course, but if you like to start the new year off with a clear head then this is a word well worth remembering. Derived from the same Roman goddess whose name inspired **matutolypea** (which is very much this word's opposite), the adjective *matutinal* was initially used much more loosely in English to refer to anything relating to or occurring in the period just after waking. By the nineteenth century, however, it had gained a more personal application, referring to an energetic early-riser's feeling of alertness or vigour.

newry's-morn (*n.*) the morning of New Year's Day [dial., 1896; < *newry, newery*, 'new year's']

Best to start the morning of 1 January off well because, according to folklore, whatever you do first thing on *newry's-morn* – the morning of New Year's Day – you'll continue to do for much of the rest of the year.

pollicitation (*n.*) the act of making a promise [15thC; < Lat. *pollicitari*, 'to promise']

Depending on how determined you are to see through your New Year's resolution, this may well be a word that comes in handy on New Year's Eve. The act of breaking a solemn promise, meanwhile, is **fedifraction**, while proverbially 'to be John at night but Jack in the morning' is to make promises at night that you go back on next day.

See also **hearthstone talk**, **velleity**

qualtagh (*n.*) the first person you meet or who enters your home on New Year's morning [1835; < Manx *quaail*, 'a meeting, a coming together']

If you think that word looks too unruly even for the madcap spelling of English, you'd be quite right: *qualtagh*, or *quaaltagh*, is a word adopted from Manx, the Celtic-origin language of the Isle of Man. At its root is a Manx word, *quaail*, for a meeting or act of coming together, and as such *qualtagh* was originally used in its native Manx merely of an assembly of festive mummers or entertainers, who would convene at Christmas or New Year to go carolling and gambolling from door to door.

> *A company of young lads or men, generally went in old times on what they termed the Qualtagh, at Christmas or New Year's Day to the house of their more wealthy neighbours.*
>
> Archibald Cregeen, *A Dictionary of the Manks Language* (1835)

Having given their performance, the qualtagh entertainers were then invited into the home, 'to partake of the best that the house could afford'. And as all of this tended to happen on New Year's Day, naturally the ringleader of the qualtagh often involuntarily became the household's first-footer – that is, the first person to cross the home's threshold in the new year. Consequently, the meaning of the word *qualtagh* shifted over time, to refer not to these entertainers as a group but to the very first of them to enter or be encountered outside a house. Thanks to a quirk of local folklore, however, in these instances there was an unusual catch:

> *It was considered fortunate if the qualtagh were a person (a man being preferred to a woman), of dark complexion, as meeting a person of light complexion at this time, especially if his or her hair is red, would be thought very unlucky.*
>
> A. W. Moore, *The Folk-Lore of the Isle of Man* (1891)

The tradition that a first-footer or *qualtagh* should be dark-haired is by no means unique to the Isle of Man, and variations of this theme can be found across Scotland, Ireland and northern England (**lucky-bird**). One popular theory claims that the festive veto on blondes and redheads is a hangover from the days of the Viking invasions, when the sight of a fair-haired stranger approaching the door to a home could understandably spell trouble, or else an enduring reference to Jesus's betrayal by Judas Iscariot, who is popularly said to have had red hair.

resolutionist (*n.*) someone who makes a New Year's resolution [1909; < *resolution* + *–ist*]

Unsurprisingly, this word was originally applied to anyone who made or supported any kind of formal resolution, but in the early 1900s it came to refer particularly (and rather unseriously) to someone who makes a New Year's resolution. Happily, the term still stands, even if your resolution might not.

velleity (*n.*) a desire or wish that you make no real attempt to achieve or pursue [1624; < Lat. *velle*, 'to wish']

Once you've decided on a New Year's resolution, there's just the small matter of following it through. Alas, if you've set the bar a little too high for yourself, then it may end up as little more than a *velleity*. Derived from the Latin word for a wish, despite appearances this is an etymological cousin of words like *volition*, *voluntary* and – in the sense of wishing good or bad on a person – both *benevolence* and *malevolence*.

***vita nuova* (*n.*) a fresh start in life, a new beginning [It., 1934; lit. 'new life']**

To say that this expression dates from 1934 is a little disingenuous, admittedly, given that its popularity as a stock phrase can be traced back to the title of a work by the Italian poet Dante written in 1294. From there, however, it took around seven centuries for *vita nuova* to fall into wider use in English as a general expression for a new direction or start in a person's life (and more especially one following a transformative or deeply affecting experience). If you've had a rocky year and are looking forward with more hope than trepidation, ultimately, then perhaps 1 January represents the start of the *vita nuova* you have been waiting for.

watchnight (*n.*) the evening of New Year's Eve [? 19thC]

Watchnight is effectively a literal interpretation of the Latin word *vigil*, and in some Christian denominations has for centuries been used of late-night church services held on New Year's Eve, or else towards the end of the festive liturgical season. By the later nineteenth century, however, the term had begun to escape some of its more formal ecclesiastical connotations, and became a byword for the night of New Year's Eve itself.

yeresyeve (*n.*) a New Year gift [1194; < ME lit. 'year's-give']

Yeresyeve is a long-forgotten medieval word that seems to have all but dwindled out of use in the 1400s. As well as meaning a New Year's present, it appears also to have been used of gifts or bonuses bestowed at the beginning of a year on people in public office or some similar formal position – and, perhaps through the often not-quite-so-upstanding behaviour of those elevated to such positions, appears to have gained a somewhat unwelcome association with being a gift given as a bribe or inducement.

> *Jeresgive; a bribe given to the king's, or other officers, for connivance, and being favourable in their several offices.*
>
> Henry Thomas, *The Ancient Remains . . . of the City of London* (Vol 2, 1830)

11. SNOWMELT

At long last, winter is receding. The days are lengthening, the temperatures are lifting, the snow is melting and every day the sun is rising a little bit higher in the sky. Even the birds singing in the trees and the snowdrops gingerly appearing out of the ground seem to agree that there is definitely something in the air: spring is on its way.

This final set of words is concerned with this extraordinary period of change and regrowth, in which the world outside reawakens and readies itself for a new year of activity. Winter is not quite a distant memory yet, of course – the weather in the springtime can be notoriously changeable. So, alongside all the words for warming sunshine, returning birds and reappearing spring flowers, there is also a handful of terms here for deceptively late snows and delayed frosts – a wintry sting in the tail in this early spring period.

afterwinter (*n.*) a period of cold, wintry weather when spring is due or expected [1593]

When the spring doesn't return quite when planned (or even worse, the weather breaks and warms before unceremoniously plunging back below zero for a few days), then you have an *afterwinter*. This unwelcome seasonal return to the recent past is also known as a *back-winter* or *second-winter*.

apricity (*n.*) the warmth of the sun on a winter's day [1623; < Lat. *apricus*, 'sunny, warmed by the sun']

Derived from a Latin root essentially meaning 'sunniness', *apricity* is a word that has in recent years found a new life for itself online in memes and galleries of beautiful, if long-forgotten, words. Perhaps odd then that there is scarcely any record of it prior to its twenty-first century resurrection on the world wide web: the English dictionary writer Henry Cockeram – who defined *apricity* as 'the warmeness of the sunne in winter' back in 1623 – seems to have made the word up himself.

blackthorn winter (*n.*) an unexpected cold snap occurring when blackthorn trees are in blossom [1793]

Blackthorn trees tend to blossom around March and April, and hence a sudden and unseasonable cold snap around this time is known as a *blackthorn winter*. In the USA, this is more commonly known as a *blackberry winter* or a *whippoorwill winter*, the latter in reference to the arrival of migratory whippoorwill birds in the northeast from their wintering grounds in the southern states and Central America.

blue-bore (*n.*) a sudden clear blue opening in an otherwise gloomy or overcast sky [1808; *blue* + *bore*, 'hole, perforation']

As winter's grey skies at long last start to clear in the spring, you might well find a *blue-bore* breaking through above you. Said to be a sign of fine weather to come, a blue-bore opening in the sky towards the end of winter not only forecasts what lies ahead in the next few hours, but gives a tantalising glimpse of the blue skies and better spring weather in the days and weeks to come.

brachychimous (*adj.*) descriptive of having a short winter [1931; < *brachy–* (< Gk. *brachus*, 'short') + Gk. *cheimon*, 'winter']

In some years, spring arrives early and you find yourself out and about in fine weather having not endured much of a winter at all.

Just such a year or season could be labelled as *brachychimous* – a word first used in botanical parlance to describe the effect of such washout winters on gardens and plants.

breard (*n.*) the first growth of a plant visible above the earth [16thC; < OE *brerd*, 'point, topmost part']

If your heart sings when you spot the first fresh green growth peeking out above the soil in the springtime, then what you're on the lookout for is a *breard*. Although, in this context at least, it has been in use since the mid 1500s, its origins lie in a far earlier Old English word, *brerd*, for the very topmost point, part or surface of something.

See also **greenout**

chelidonian (*adj.*) of a breeze in the early spring: noticeably warm and blowing from the southwest [1625; < Gk. *chelidon*, 'swallow']

The first noticeably warm breeze of the springtime is a *chelidonian* breeze. Taking its name from the Greek word for a swallow, this warm south to south-westerly wind was so called because it was once widely believed either to carry or assist the birds as they completed their migration north from Africa, or else simply to coincide with the arrival of the first swallows of the springtime as they returned to European skies after the winter.

chionophile (*n.*) something that thrives in the snow, or that needs snow cover in order to thrive in the spring [1902; < Gk. *chion*, 'snow' + *–phile* (< Gk. *philos*, 'beloved, loving')]

Literally meaning a 'snow-lover', this term may well apply to you, of course, but in zoological and botanical contexts it is more typically used of animals and plants that are not only well adapted to see their way through the winter months, but actively need wintry conditions in order to do so. Polar bears and seals need the thick layers of ice on which to hunt and raise their pups, for instance, while some trees and other plants need an annual period of cold weather in order to trigger them to bloom and come into fruit in the spring.

devil's smiles (*n. pl.*) periods of unstable or unpredictable weather, alternating between sunshine and showers, at the end of winter or early spring [1867; ? < the deceptiveness of the weather]

As temperatures rise and the days grow longer, the weather can become wetter and less predictable in the early springtime, which makes *devil's smiles* a more frequent occurrence. As well as referring to alternating periods of sun and rain, in nineteenth-century naval English a *devil's smile* was a deceptive glimpse of bright sunshine in an otherwise stormy or overcast sky (or, according to an 1885 guide to *Legends and Superstitions of the Sea*, 'the scowl on an angry captain's face').

eving, eaving (*v., adj.*) of ice: just beginning to thaw or release moisture [1777; ? < *give*, 'to yield']

Eve, or *eave*, has been in regional use in English since at least the eighteenth century as a verb meaning to become moist or dewy with condensation; etymologically, it is thought to be effectively a G-less form of *give*. In relation to winter weather in particular, however, *eaving* is the gradual release of fresh water from ice, frost or snow as they begin to melt. And as the winter turns to spring, that's something that will no doubt become ever more commonplace.

farewell fieldfare (*excl.*) **'goodbye and good riddance!' [14thC]**

Fieldfares are birds in the thrush family. Although found across much of continental Europe all year round, in Britain they are winter visitors and arrive in fairly large numbers from Scandinavia each year to escape the harsher weather further north. Then, having seeing out the winter months in the relatively mild British Isles, the birds depart again for the northern European mainland in the spring.

This coming and going either side of winter is what lies behind this curious expression – equivalent to 'Good riddance!' or 'You won't be missed!' – which has been in recorded use since medieval times. As inadvertent symbols of the winter and bad weather, the departure of the fieldfares in spring was seen as heralding the milder and brighter weather ahead, and so understandably became something to be celebrated.

floriage (*n.*) **a blossoming or blooming [1782; ultimately < Lat.** ***flos*****, 'flower']**

When blossom trees begin to flower in the springtime, the colourful display they put on can be known collectively as their *floriage*. Derived from a Latin word for a flower, this is an etymological cousin of more familiar terms like *floral*, *florist*, *flourish* and *efflorescence*.

frondescentia (*n.*) **the season or time of year when flowers bloom and trees produce new leaves [1796; partly < Lat.** ***frons*****, 'leaf']**

The Latin *frons*, meaning a leaf, is the origin of a host of botanical and technical terms, including *frondescent* ('producing leaves'), *frondiferous* ('bearing leaves') and *frondesce* ('to grow leaves').

According to a 1796 guide to the *Language of Botany*, meanwhile, *frondescentia* is 'the time of year when plants first unfold their leaves' and come into bloom and bud in the spring.

gandays (*n.*) the last fortnight of winter and the first fortnight of spring [Sc. 1825; < lit. 'going days']

The period known as the *gandays*, or *gaundays*, is literally the winter's 'going-days', when the season is at long last on its way out and the spring can finally be welcomed in. That being said, it has been suggested that this phrase may have been inspired by (or may even have originally referred to) the three so-called Rogation Days of prayer and fasting in the church calendar that preceded Ascension Day, thirty-nine days after Easter. If that is the case, then the 'going' in the *gandays* might not be the disappearance of winter, but a reference to the 'going' of religious processioners around a church parish.

glisk (*n.*) a brief passing glimpse of warm sunshine [1820; of unknown origin, ? < Scan.]

In general terms, a *glisk* is a short peek or glance at something, but since the 1700s the word has been recorded in a handful of more figurative senses relating to all manner of momentary occurrences – from a fright or unwelcome surprise to a brief frisson of pleasure, a pang of guilt and even an unwelcome whiff of a bad smell.

In relation to the weather, a *glisk* is a similarly momentary spell of bright or warm sunshine, and in particular one that breaks only passingly through thick grey cloud – just the kind of enticing yet frustrating glimmer of springtime that might all too briefly pass by on an otherwise murky day at the end of winter.

gloor (*v.*) **of the sun: to shine weakly through haze or small breaks in the cloud [Sc., 1908; of unknown origin]**

As a noun, a *gloor* is a spell of 'warm sunshine after rain', according to the *Scottish National Dictionary*, while as a verb it describes the only faint shining of hazy sunshine on an otherwise overcast day.

goor (*n.*) **half-melted snow or ice [Sc., dial., 1866; ? < ON** *gor*, **'sludge, cud']**

Thought to be related to or even descended from a Scandinavian word for wet mud or sludge, *goor* is the sloppy slush of partly melted snow (used only, according to the *English Dialect Dictionary*, of that which ends up in streams, rivers and other running water). If a stream becomes *goored*, meanwhile, then it becomes choked with such a quantity of slushy snowmelt that its flow slows or becomes blocked altogether.

greenout (*n.*) **the feeling of gladness or relief that a person who has endured the winter experiences on seeing something fresh and green for the first time [Antarctic sl., 1996]**

If the winter has been an especially hard or long one, then the sight of the first snowdrops or crocuses breaking through the snowy ground – or the first leaves or buds on the trees as spring begins to creep through – can come as a considerable relief. That feeling is called *greenout*, a term coined among polar research scientists (whose experience of a decidedly greenless and lifeless winter must surely be even more stark than our own).

gruft (*n.*) dusty particles of soil that are lifted by rain among blades of grass [1803; of unknown origin]

As any keen gardener will no doubt tell you, the action of frost and ice, and the repeated freezing and thawing of the ground throughout the winter months, can have a disastrous effect on the soil. Cold air can make the ground dry and brittle, while the coming and going of layers of frost can break the earth up into fine powdery flakes. When the snow and ice finally give way to rain, this powdery material, known as *gruft*, can then be lifted up from the ground by the rain, and can often be seen floating on the surface of pools and puddles of rainwater.

lamb-blast (*n.*) a spring snowstorm or thunderstorm [dial., 1889]

Rainy or blustery periods of unsettled weather in the early spring, often accompanied by cold north-easterly winds, are known as *lamb-blasts*. The name refers to the fact that these noticeably chilly squalls typically blow in around the time of the births of the year's first new lambs.

lapwing-snow (*n.*) a blast of snowy, wintry weather in the early spring [dial., 1905]

Lapwing-snow, or a *lapwing-winter*, is a period of unseasonably cold weather that coincides with the seasonal arrival of lapwing birds in isolated parts of northern and central Europe. Lapwings are resident all year round in much of the British Isles, but some birds – both here and in continental Europe – head further north and east during the milder months to breed. Such is the climate of these more northerly locations, however, that spring often starts with a whimper rather than a bang as the final snowstorms of the winter prove they still have work left to do.

new year's gift (*n.*) the buttercup *Eranthis hyemalis* [1856; < its welcome arrival in the early part of the year]

Better known as the winter aconite, this particular species of buttercup is so named because it is typically one of the year's very earliest flowering plants. Its bright yellow cup-shaped flowers can frequently be seen sprouting close to the earth in fields and woodlands, often when there is still snow or frost on the ground.

opetide (*n.*) the early spring [1597; < lit. 'opening time']

The name *opetide*, or *opentide*, has been used since medieval times to refer to various periods throughout the year when certain rules or restrictions were lifted, or not imposed. The earliest recorded *opetide* in this sense dates back to the early 1200s, when the name was given to the fastless period in the church calendar (outside of Lent). Over the centuries it has also been used of a post-harvest season in the autumn (when cattle can be returned to open fields) and a legal period between Epiphany and Ash Wednesday (when marriages could traditionally be openly and freely announced). In all of these senses, 'open' is meant to imply free access or a lack of constraints or restrictions, but in the sixteenth century the term picked up an additional sense as a name for the very earliest period of spring – so called because it is then that buds and flowers first begin to open.

perennate (*v.*) to survive from one season to the next [? 19thC; < Lat. *perennare*, 'to endure, to last']

To *perennate* is essentially to become perennial – that is, to last or survive a great many years – and it was in that more literal sense that this word first appeared in the language in the 1600s.

Since around the turn of the last century, however, words like *perennate* and *perennial* have much more familiarly come to be used of flowers and plants that appear to die off before the winter, see out the toughest season in a state of dormancy and then bud and bloom again in the spring. In this sense, the word can be used to mean simply to survive or to see out the winter months – which, if you have made it this far, is precisely what you've done.

prevernal (*adj.*) relating to the late winter or early spring [1877; < *pre–* + *vernal*, 'of the spring']

The Latin word for spring was *ver*, and it is from there that the *vernal* equinox takes its name (as well as the Italian *primavera*). Derived from the same root is *prevernal*, a somewhat obscure and literary adjective dating from the late 1800s, which refers to the period either immediately before the spring, or in the very early part of it.

> *O, quick, praevernal Power*
> *That signall'st punctual through the sleepy mould*
> *The Snowdrop's time to flower.*
>
> Coventry Patmore, 'St Valentine's Day' (1877)

See also **vernalagnia**

repullulate (*v.*) to regrow or come into flower once more [1608; partly < *re–* + Lat. *pullus*, 'chick']

Derived from a Latin word, *pullus*, for a chick or the young of an animal, to *pullulate* is to grow or come into existence, so to *repullulate* is to regrow or sprout anew.

reverdie (*n.*) a song or poem celebrating the return of spring [1896; < Fr. *reverdir*, 'to become green again']

Although it only appeared in English in the Victorian era, in its native French the word *reverdie* has been in use since medieval times to refer to some manner of literary or musical work written to celebrate the return of spring.

routering-bout (*n.*) a spring-clean [1876; < *routering*, 'rushing around' + *bout*, 'spell, session']

To *router*, or *rooter*, is to rush around noisily or, in the words of the *English Dialect Dictionary*, 'to make a search amidst a confusion of things'. In the sense of perhaps doing both of those things at once, a *routering-bout* is a thorough spring-clean.

> *Routering time, or a routering bout . . . the annual spring period for the housewife's 'dust-fever', when every article, from the cellar to the attic, undergoes a thorough purgation.*
>
> John Harland, *A Glossary of Words Used in Swaledale, Yorkshire* (1876)

shurl (*n.*) a slide of snow from the roof of a house [Sc., 1911; < earlier *shirl*, *shurl*, 'slip, slide']

'A glissade of accumulated snow from a roof after a thaw' is how the *Scottish National Dictionary* defines a *shurl*, which may be one of the most noticeable and noisiest signs yet of the oncoming spring. Etymologically, the word *shurl*, or *shirl*, has been used for centuries in various senses relating to a smooth gliding or sliding movement, of which this is just one: a slip on an icy surface can also be called a *shirl*, and so too can the imperceptible sliding by of time, and a shuffling, prevaricating excuse (especially one that acts as a loophole that lets you 'slide' out of an unwelcome deal or arrangement).

snow-broth (*n.*) water made from or released by melting snow [1600; < *snow* + *broth*, 'stew, potage']

As well as referring to natural meltwater released by gradually rising temperatures, calling this liquid a 'broth' hints at the fact that snow was also apparently used as a source of fresh water: 'Snow melted in a vessel' is the definition of *snow-broth* given in an 1862 dictionary of *The Dialect of Leeds*. In nineteenth-century American English, meanwhile, the term came to be used more figuratively of cold liquor, or a draft of alcoholic drink that – unlike brandy or whisky – does not provide a warming boost.

spring fever (*n.*) a springtime feeling of listlessness, restlessness or romance [1843]

See **vernalagnia**

spring fret (*n.*) a feeling of restlessness or a desire to travel or wander sparked by the return of the fine weather in the spring [1897; < *spring* + *fret*, 'moment of mental agitation']

When spring at long last breaks after the cold and dull winter months, it can spark a restless wanderlust in even the least outdoorsy of people. If you find yourself eager to get outside once the sun is shining and the temperatures are rising, then perhaps you're experiencing *spring fret*.

sunbreak (*n.*) a burst of warm sunshine on an otherwise cloudy or overcast day [1826]

As well as being another word for sunrise (modelled on the far older *daybreak*), a *sunbreak* can also be a sudden burst of sunny warmth or light that literally 'breaks' through an otherwise gloomy or grey sky.

turn of the year (*n.*) the end of winter and the beginning of spring [1637]

We might be more inclined to think of the *turn of the year* as being 1 January, but this expression was formerly used more of the turning of the seasons, when the harsh weather of the wintertime began to slacken and the brighter (though still somewhat nippy) spring took its place.

> *Who doesn't know the chilling feel of an English spring, or rather of a day at the turn of the year before there is any spring? . . . A white frost, succeeded by a bright sun, with an east wind, warming one side of the face and starving the other.*
>
> R. S. Surtees, *Mr. Sponge's Sporting Tour* (1853)

valentining (*n.*, *v.*) the singing of mating birds in the spring [1855; < *valentine*, 'romantic message']

Regrettably this is not an official ornithological expression (or at least not yet), but rather a poetic turn of phrase established in the romantic era of the nineteenth century. Alfred, Lord Tennyson first used the word *valentine* to refer to a bird's springtime mating in his 1847 poem 'The Princess':

> *Beneath huge trees, a thousand rings of Spring*
> *In every bole, a song on every spray*
> *Of birds that piped their Valentines*

And perhaps inspired by him, several later poets of the same era followed suit, establishing *valentine* as a verb meaning 'to greet with song . . . at mating-time', according to the *Oxford English Dictionary*.

vernalagnia (*n.*) a romantic mood brought on by the return of fine weather in the spring [1958; < Lat. *ver*, spring + Gk. *lagneia*, 'lust']

If the warm spring weather, sunshine, birdsong and newly budding trees all conspire to put you in a romantic frame of mind, then you're suffering a bout of *vernalagnia*. Despite some impressive Latin and Greek roots, this appears to be a fairly recent coinage, seemingly found in print no earlier than the mid twentieth century. The feeling of post-winter friskiness it describes is nothing new, however, and has been rather less romantically known as **spring fever** since the 1800s.

Unfortunately, as well as lacking the classical chops of *vernalagnia*, the name *spring fever* has the added disadvantage of originally being the name of an actual disease, variously identified as anything from a kind of warm-weather ague, accompanied by dysentery-like symptoms, to a scurvy-like deficiency caused by a lack of fresh fruit during the winter months. Perhaps best to plump for *vernalagnia*, then, to describe this springtime spring in your step, given that there must surely be few things more likely to put an end to a feeling of friskiness than an unexpected bout of dysentery.

vernality (*n.*) the spring, a spring-like quality; the greenness and freshness of springtime [1896; ultimately < Lat. *ver*, 'spring']

As well as referring to the collective qualities and characteristics of spring, *vernality* can also be used more figuratively of an early period of development or flourishment.

weather-breeder (*n.*) an unseasonably warm day in February [1895; < *weather* + *breeder*, in the sense of something that produces or generates]

One of the first signs of the ongoing spring is a day, still in the depths of winter, when the temperature outside suddenly spikes, and the winter hat, scarf, gloves and coat can all be left in the cupboard. Since the 1800s, just such a day has been known as a *weather-breeder* – especially if it happens to fall amid a longer or more protracted period of stormy or wintry weather. According to local folklore, meanwhile, if a weather-breeder falls in February, then it is said to forecast an early spring and warm, fine weather to come.

Other explanations and definitions give a slightly different account of what a *weather-breeder* is or is meant to portend, however: over the decades and in different dialect regions the term has been applied to all kinds of weather phenomena said to forecast a change ahead. A bright beam of sunshine on an overcast day, for instance, can also be called a *weather-breeder*, as can the warmth or humidity that precedes a thunderstorm, and a noticeably dark and isolated cloud (the appearance of which was once supposed to forecast rain).

> *Intervals of pleasant weather occasionally brighten the face of Nature, and the sunlight flings the shadows of the trees distinctly upon the land, and we are tempted forth to lengthy rambles . . . There is scarcely a breath of wind, and the rays of the morning sun are dazzling after days of storm and mist and gloom.*
>
> *'Ah! 'bor – ' volunteers a son of old Ocean . . . 'This here's only a waather-breeder.'*
>
> Arthur Patterson, *Man and Nature on the Broads* (1895)

whicken (*v.*) of the days: to lengthen in the spring; of the year or the world itself: to recover from the harsh winter months [1876; < *quicken*, 'come to life']

Before it meant speedy or rapid, the word *quick* meant living, and so to *whicken* (which is a regional variant of *quicken* recorded in a number of English dialects) literally means to come to life. In the dialects of Yorkshire in particular, according to one 1876 definition, this was a term used 'in reference to the lengthening of days and the revival of vegetation in spring' to mean 'to awake from the death of winter' – making it an optimal word for the arrival of the springtime, and a fitting final entry in our dictionary of winter.

ACKNOWLEDGEMENTS

Thanks as always to Pippa Crane, Sarah Rigby and all at Elliott & Thompson for suggesting the idea behind this book, and to my agent, Andrew Lownie, for his tireless efforts in putting it into motion.

This book would not exist without the dictionary writers and lexicographers – both past and present – whose books and glossaries recorded the words I merely had to bring together here. If you have enjoyed this collection, there is far more gold to be mined in their work.

Thanks also to Owen Nutt, Matthew Norris and Reece Lau for their help in keeping this book (and its author) on the right track. We can organise another *powl* sometime soon.

WORD FINDER

D

ALSO BY PAUL ANTHONY JONES

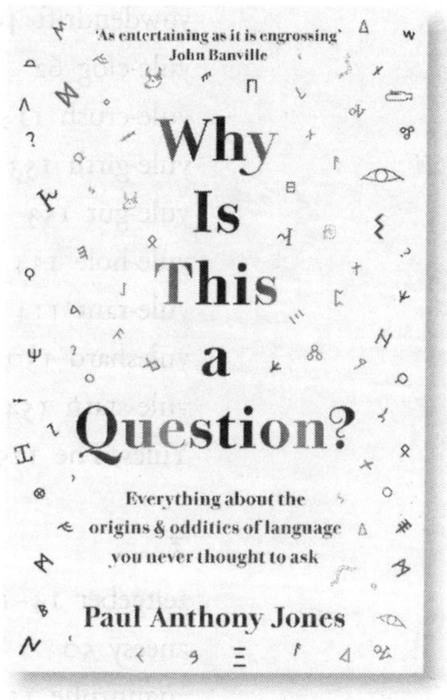

'As entertaining as it is engrossing.'
John Banville

'Enlightening, delightful.'
Arthur der Weduwen, author of *The Library*

Why don't eleven and twelve end in –teen? Why are some letters uppercase and others lowercase? Why are these words in this order? And what is this question mark really doing at the end of this sentence?

Why Is This a Question? is a fascinating and enlightening exploration of linguistic questions you've likely never thought to ask, delving into the origins of our alphabet and writing system; grammatical rules and conventions; the sound structure of language; and even how our brains and bodies interpret and communicate language itself.

ISBN: 978-1-78396-702-5

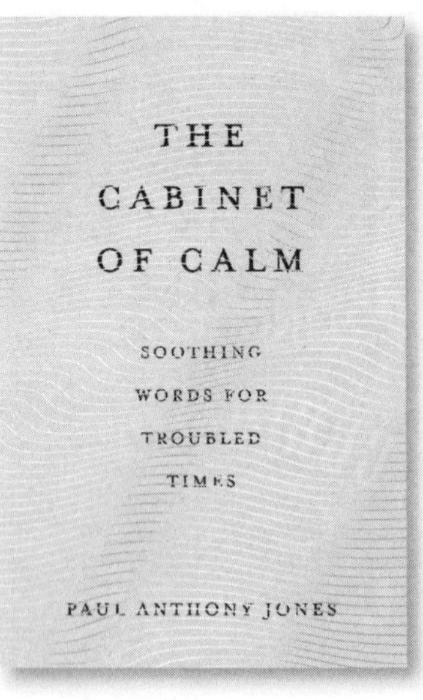

'Fantastic . . . Exactly the book that everybody needs.'
Simon Mayo

Open *The Cabinet of Calm* to discover a comforting word that's equal to your troubles.

With fifty-one soothing words for troubled times, whenever you need a moment of serenity, just select the emotion listed that reflects what you're feeling and you'll be offered a matching linguistic remedy to bring peace, comfort and delight, and provide fresh hope.

So much more than a book of words, *The Cabinet of Calm* will soothe your soul and ease your mind.

ISBN: 978-1-78396-592-2

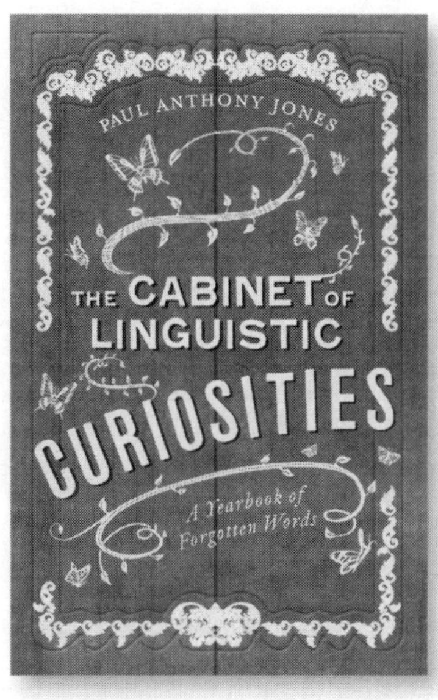

The Cabinet of Linguistic Curiosities contains a wealth of strange and forgotten words for every day of the year. Dip into this beautiful book to be delighted and intrigued throughout the year as you learn about linguistic trivia, follow a curious thread or wonder at the web of connections in the English language.

1 January **quaaltagh** (n.) the first person you meet on New Year's Day

1 April **dorbellist** (n.) a fool, a dull-witted dolt

12 May **word-grubber** (n.) someone who uses obscure or difficult words in everyday conversation

25 September **theic** (adj.) an excessive drinker of tea

24 December **doniferous** (adj.) carrying a gift

ISBN: 978-1-78396-439-0

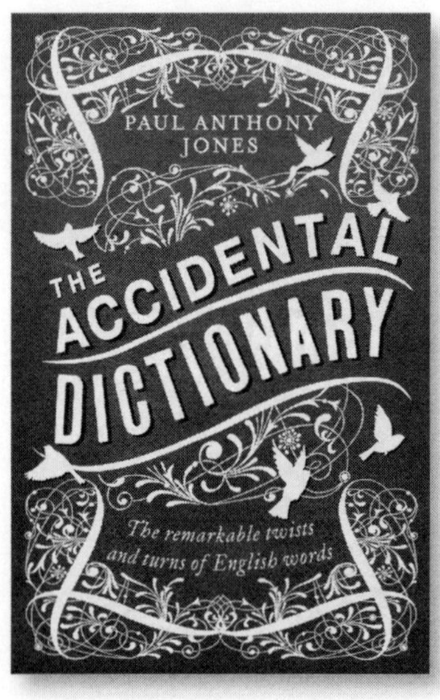

Buxom used to mean *obedient*
A *cloud* was a *rock*
Raunchy originally meant *dirty*

Our everyday language is full of surprises; its origins are stranger than you might think. Any word might be knocked and buffeted, subjected to twists and turns, expansions and contractions, happy and unhappy accidents. There are intriguing tales behind even the most familiar terms, and they can say as much about the present as they do the past.

Brimming with hidden histories and tantalising twists, *The Accidental Dictionary* tells the extraordinary stories behind ordinary words.

ISBN: 978-1-78396-438-3

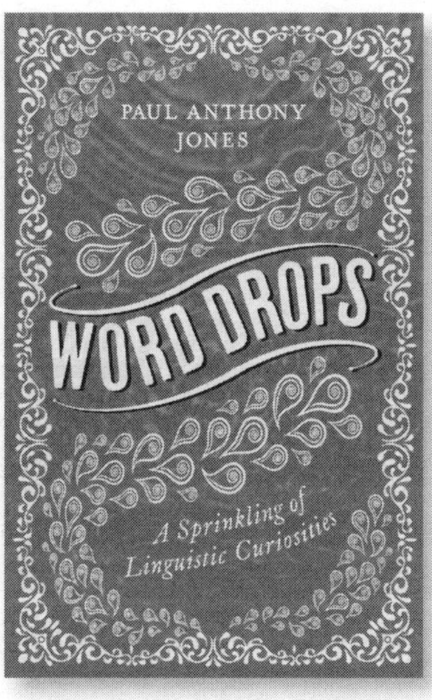

To *grin* originally meant 'to show your teeth'.
An *eccedentesiast* is someone who fakes a smile.
A *much-faker* is someone who mends umbrellas.
Impluvious means 'utterly soaked with rain'.

Word Drops is a language fact book unlike any other, its linguistic tidbits all falling together into one long interconnected chain just like the examples above, with each fact neatly 'dropping' into place beside the next.

This surprising compendium of 1,000 facts about words, language and etymology is here to inspire your curiosity and delight in discovery. For all of the *logofascinated* among us, this is an immensely pleasurable and unpredictable collection that is guaranteed to raise eyebrows (the literal meaning, incidentally, of *supercilious*).

ISBN: 978-1-78396-437-6

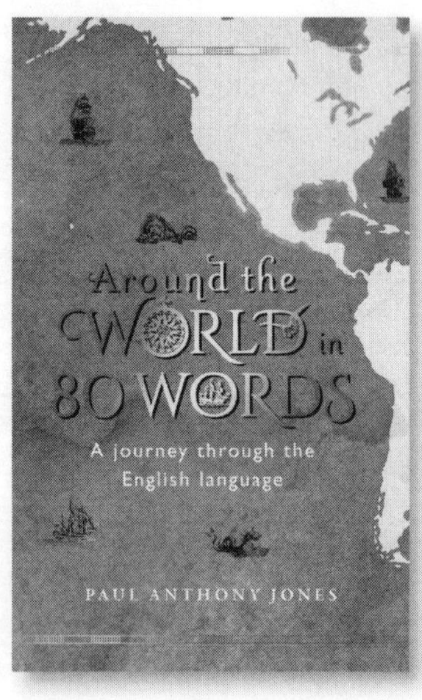

From Monte Carlo to Shanghai, Bikini to Samarra, *Around the World in 80 Words* is a whimsical voyage through the far-flung reaches of the English language, revealing the intriguing stories of how 80 different places came to be immortalised in our language.

Beginning in London and heading through Europe, Africa, Asia, Australia and the Americas, you'll discover the origins of turkeys, Brazil nuts, limericks and Panama hats; what an island with more bears than people has given to your liquor cabinet; and how a tiny hamlet in Nottinghamshire became Gotham City.

Surprising and consistently entertaining, this is essential reading for armchair travellers and word nerds. Our dictionaries are full of hidden histories, tales and adventures from all over the world – if you know where to look.

ISBN: 978-1-78396-400-0